Mat. 10 —

Compliments

W. J. Geandron

April 18th 1922.

The Destiny of America

"There is a principle which is a bar against all information, which is proof against all argument, and which cannot fail to keep man in everlasting ignorance. This principle is contempt prior to examination".—*Dr. Paley.*

A greater than Paley has said: "He that answereth a matter before he heareth it, it is a folly, and a shame unto him.—*Proverbs XVIII.* 13.

The Destiny of America

WITH AN APPENDIX

Who Are The Japanese?

BY

THE ROADBUILDER

Wm G. MacKendrick

BOSTON, MASS.:
A. A. BEAUCHAMP,
603 BOYLSTON ST.

320.56
M155d

Copyright, Canada, 1921
By
T. H. BEST PRINTING CO., LTD.
All Rights Reserved.

RESPECTFULLY DEDICATED

TO

THE SHORT-HAIRED BUSINESS MEN
OF AMERICA,

Men, Chuck Full of Sentiment, Enterprise and Goodwill who, given facts, can usually deliver an intelligent opinion and judgment quicker, it is alleged, than "hell can scorch a feather."

Having never been nearer hell than France and Belgium during war-time, I am unable to say if the above time limit is a reasonable one, but cheerfully and with confidence I submit the following facts, history, statements, and deductions, both Biblical and profane, to your mature business judgment, well knowing that they will be dealt with by a fifty-fifty mixture of grey matter and horse sense, which is all one could ask.

THE ROADBUILDER.

October, 1920. *Col. Wm. Gordon MacKendrick*
1864—

THE OBJECTIVE.

Our fighting troops in France and Flanders, after several years warfare and at the cost of many thousands of lives, learned that a limited objective properly planned was the one thing necessary before leading troops "over the top."

This lesson remains seared somewhere in my interior economy; and before leading you across what might be called a "No Man's Land," it might be well to explain that the objective at present in view is to cause you business men of the U.S.A., citizens of the greatest republic the world ever has seen, or ever will see, to look into some facts of history that in so many unmistakable ways seem to connect your country with the promises made by God through the mouths of His prophets several thousand years ago, foretelling the great people you were to become as descendants of Manasseh, the eldest son of Joseph, whom you will remember as the food controller who saved not only Egypt and his Hebrew brethren but the world at large, for it is stated, "The famine was over all the face of the earth. . . . And all countries came into Egypt to Joseph for to buy corn."

It is hoped with this limited objective in view to secure your interest and goodwill sufficiently to cause you to study the subject, though I must advise you before you start that, when you study it, you're a "gonner"! The theme is so captivating, the side lines so many, and every one so interesting that your golf or other pursuits are apt to be neglected while you delve for data as to what is going to be the outcome of the present unsettled condition of Europe, of America, and the whole world, because it is all foretold in Bible history, which I like to call *His*-story, *i.e.,* God's story. The dime novels of your youthful days were no more thrilling than is this subject to every man who has looked into it carefully; and the more and the deeper you delve, the richer the plunder.

This limited objective, therefore, is only to provide you with a jumping-off spot or bridgehead for the real attack you will make when you have absorbed the fact that God selected America for you and foretold through the mouths of the prophets of old, the "people" and the "great people" you were to become.

When away from home, you speak of the U.S.A. as God's own country; and you do well, for in Psalms 60: we read: "God hath spoken in his holiness. . . . Manasseh is Mine," and the U.S.A. is Manasseh. You and your country are His, as I hope you will agree, if you have the patience to wade through the following pages.

It surely will not make you think less of your country to know that the Creator in His plan for this world selected America for you to grow up in and become the freedom-loving people you are. It will not make you think less of your national inheritance and the Anglo-Saxon-Celtic-British stock from which you sprang to learn that God foretold, through the mouths of His prophets several thousand years ago, that you were to break away and set up in business for yourselves and from a little one you would grow into a great nation; and that you would, like Brother John Bull, be invincible in war; and that He would give you both the wealth of the mine, the forest, the sea, and the wealth of the land,—all of which has made Young America the wonder of the world, and has thus enabled you to help do His work with wealth at your command.

God also laid down the specifications for the job you were to help to do in this world: in freeing the slaves, in breaking all yokes, and in helping to carry His Word and good works to all nations together with that British love of freedom and justice that forms a part of your inheritance from your forefathers.

If any of your immediate forefathers had left you the one-thousandth part of what God bequeathed to you and your fathers as an inheritance, you would be breaking your neck to find out all about it, so I hope this prospect will not leave you "cold footed."

FOREWORD.

Say, reader, did you ever write a book? No! Well, neither have I, so we break even on that score.

When I came back from the Front in the spring of 1919, I had a decided hunch that I should put on paper these views for the benefit of my numerous Yankee friends and perhaps for a few others. Now, a brain wave to most people is a creature of a moment or two and then passes off, but with this bit of Scotch it is a real force to be reckoned with and to be humored, or got rid of, or else followed.

Choosing the latter course, I started to put on paper these ideas, but I found that when I commenced looking up any of the reference books or the Bible, I at once became so interested in reading—and I read night after night and never put a page on paper—that my writing languished. Besides, I realized I was never made to sit still long enough for quill driving and my mental equipment was unsuited for such work, for, be it known, the call of the "out of doors" at the age of thirteen caused me to play "hookey" for several months (there being no truant officers in those days) and my young form darkened school doors no more.

I also soon recognized that this was essentially a religious question; and while I have been accused of many things, up to date I have never heard of my being accused of being pious or religious, as I have never felt good enough to join a church, though I once had the compliment passed by a very reverend gentleman asking me to be a sidesman, deacon or churchwarden, I don't remember which. But I was not for having any, though I attend service every Sunday, rain or shine.

Amid these discouragements, the calls of business with a turn-over of two million dollars, and the thronging duties that fall to one's portion in a big city, absorbed a good deal of my steam, so that when I reached home in the evening, it was slippers, a grate fire, a game of bridge, and a growing family that took my attention ere the feathers wooed me thitherward.

My conscience or the aforementioned hunch, however, never lost its grip but kept urging me on despite the numerous times I waved it aside with many a "to-morrow perhaps," or "next week."

Sitting one day in the Club after luncheon, talking to a young friend of about sixty-five or seventy summers and an equal number of winters, mostly hard ones I should judge, we chanced on this subject and I unloaded some of the following data off my chest.

Turning to me with real passion in his voice, he said, "I would give anything in the world that I possess if I had your faith!"

"Say, Tom, it's not that costly! Just invest a few dollars in some books I'll give you a list of, and I'll bet you cannot come to any other conclusion than I have."

Turning to me with real earnestness, he said,

"The world is just crying out for the faith that you have; and you would be doing more real service and good than you could estimate if you would publish what you have just told me, as you have a way of saying things that make them stick in one's mind. You would be doing a real service to humanity in renewing the faith that we were taught by our mothers in the years long ago. We need it sadly."

This talk stirred me to renewed action; so, here I am with my finger in the ink-pot under the urge of my young friend, whose opinion and judgment I value highly, trying, and trying hard, to write a book that will show you the everyday road to God's Kingdom that is right here on earth. You don't have to die to get it as it is part of your inheritance while you are alive and going strong.

Having served this notice of what to ex-

pect, I seem to have cleared my conscience, because, if you delve further into these pages, its your own funeral, as you have had fair warning that I am far removed from being properly equipped or suited to the job of bookwriting. Think of it rather as a series of letters from a friend direct to you. I'm appalled at the number of capital "I's" in the foregoing, but it seems impossible to dodge them, due doubtless to my inexperience and not knowing how.

I really have little that is *original* to offer you; but, during the last thirty-seven years, I have read over 250 books and pamphlets on this subject and the data contained therein has been absorbed during those years. My test of every book has been to check up its statements or data by the Bible, and my father might have been from Missouri, instead of from Glasgow, Scotland, by the way they had to "show me!"

It is impossible, therefore, to quote all the authors whose material I have absorbed, but when I make a statement you can bank on its being based on the good horse sense that you apply to your business daily, and you can be sure that it is *all truth* as it is given me to see it.

Furthermore, a book like this is only of as much good to you as the use you make of it; and if you desire to get anything out of it, it will have to be studied and checked up, not merely read for entertainment. I always read with a soft pencil in my hand. For every opinion expressed that I cannot see or do not believe, I put a question mark in the margin. I tick off the things I agree with or wish to refer to again. I turn down the corner of pages I wish to refer to hurriedly, and I can glance through a book a second time from cover to cover in half an hour. *I would ask as a favor that you do likewise with this book,* because to really get it, you will have to study it over many times to absorb most of the truth it contains. Question anything you cannot see or do not believe; heavily pencil any items that strike you as good stuff; and don't be afraid of digging into the Bible to do a bit of mining on your own account, as not one-half of it as yet is properly understood by most people.

You do your business six days a week on the basis of taking other men's word for details and things you have not time or inclination to go into or figure for yourself. I would ask that you do the same with me as you do with your subordinates and place the same confidence in my judgment and accept my word for everything I put down here until you finish the book and *until you find me in error,* because its facts are as true as the fact that you have a head on your shoulders.

As you may be undecided whether to accept the foregoing suggestion, I may mention that my bank backs my word and judgment to the tune of between a quarter and a half million dollars overdraft each season and they, as you know, have the habit of looking into the innermost recesses of one's make-up ere they loosen to the above tune.

Mention is made of this, not in a boastful manner, nor to encourage you to seek a loan, but solely because I think it well you should know that my head is screwed on shoulders as straight and as tight as is the ordinary business man's who has to rustle among his competitors daily for his provender in the marts of a large city.

THE ROADBUILDER.

November, 1920.

DETAILS OF CHAPTER I.

1. My early chief.
2. U.S.A. God's chosen land and people.
3. Enquiry about the war in France and Flanders.
4. Germany's aim to maim France for life.
5. Turkey's doom by Ephraim (England) foretold.
6. The mills of God grind slowly.
7. What it cost Britain for breaking of God's laws.
8. What it cost U.S.A. for breaking one of God's laws.
9. Moses and Abraham Lincoln both called to carry out God's laws.
10. Abraham Lincoln's belief that Almighty God ruled in America, but that Americans had forgotten God.
11. What it cost America for not knowing in 1861 that they were Israel.
12. The League of Nations cannot and will not stop war.
13. A league of Anglo-Saxon nations only will bring ordered peace and justice.
14. Then Schwab can scrap his armament department, not before.
15. The farseeing stockbroker vs. the farther seeing Creator.

16. God said Ephraim, Israel, would free Jerusalem from Edom, the Turk, and as Britain did so she must be Israel.
17. Where is the nation, Israel, whom Christ came to save. His ten servants whom He told to occupy His Kingdom until His return? (Luke 19).
18. Why did Christ send His Disciples to "The Lost Sheep of the House of Israel?"
19. The Creator says preachers of America have fallen down on their job and He will take it over and find "His Lost Sheep," Israel.

The Destiny of America

CHAPTER I.

Thirty years ago I was toiling in one of the large cities of Wisconsin, U.S.A., second in command of a roadbuilding company.

My chief was a young man of my own age, as fat as a match and measuring six feet two inches in his nightie (in those days pyjamas were not standard equipment for roadbuilders). This young man was a down east Yankee of, I think, the Mayflower extraction, with a strong belief and hope that the U.S.A. would finally float the Stars and Stripes from the north pole to Panama. Now, while I respected him muchly for his many charming qualities of head and heart, we, nevertheless, used to split hard and fast on the Yankee flag proposition ever floating over Canada, for, be it known, I was a "Canook" born of Scotch and English parents: on my mother's side descended from those fighting warrior Normans whom William the Conqueror led into Britain, and on my father's, from the lowland Scotch who always were bonnie fighters, wherever the cause was good—or where they thought it was, which was the same thing to them.

I had a strong working belief—namely, the Anglo-Israel theory—that the Anglo-Saxon-Celtic people headed by John Bull and Brother Jonathan were God's chosen peoples with whom He was going to subdue the heathen and whom He was going to use as His battle axe and as His weapons of war, to bring about His Kingdom on earth, according to Jeremiah 51:20:

> "Thou [Israel] art my battle axe and weapons of war: for with thee will I break in pieces the nations, and with thee will I destroy kingdoms [in and through Israel should His Kingdom be manifest on earth]."

These peoples were to be invincible in war. Their mission was to free the slaves and the oppressed, to bind up the broken, to break every yoke, to keep God's laws, to carry the Gospel to the heathen, to settle the waste places of the earth, etc., and in this way make manifest God's Kingdom right in America, Canada, Britain, and the other Anglo-Saxon nations.

Ferrar Fenton's Version in modern English of Isaiah 58:6 and 7 reads:

> "Is not this the Fast I approve?—
> To free those who are wrongfully bound?
> And to loosen your slaves from their yoke?
> And to seek out and free the oppressed?
> And that you should remove every wrong?
> And to give to the famishing food?
> And poor wanderers to bring to your house?
> And those whom you see naked to clothe?
> And to hide not yourself from your kind?"

I had been inoculated with this belief in 1884 and it had what the doctors would call a good take; but, unlike the measles, flu and a few other odds and ends that have come my way before and since and left me none the worse for their visits, this Anglo-Saxon-Celtic invasion of microbes in my system has grown until now I believe if I was scratched anywhere, I would ooze Bible prophecies concerning Israel and her future.

When my slim chief talked about God's country (the U.S.A.), I agreed that it really was God's country and belabored him with what the prophets said about America. I furthermore gave him books on the subject printed in 1879, which, by the way, predicted the taking of Egypt;—as was accomplished in 1882;—also the taking of Palestine, by Ephraim Israel (England) "doing in" Edom (Turkey); the handing of the Holy Land to the Jews for a national home under Britain; the absolute break-up of Russia; and many other things that were based on the Saxon-Celtic people alone fitting into the scheme as God's chosen people Israel—Israel later being divided into two separate Hebrew nations: Judah being the Jews, and Levi and the other ten tribes forming the nation Israel, which was lost to most historians.

Times change; and men with them. My early chief drifted to that big city of skyscrapers

—New York—and became the father of a lovely family of boys and girls, covered his bones with numerous layers of surplus tissue until a two hundred pound scale would not scale him, and the war found him general-manager of one of America's big trusts turning out munitions at a rate to surfeit his shareholders with British and French gold taken in exchange for materials for the stuffing of high explosive shells, etc.

One day in the spring of 1918, in a war-ridden section of France, my batman brought to my billet a letter that I at once recognized as the handwriting of my boss of about thirty years before. Congratulating me on my work, he wound up his epistle by asking how the war fitted into the ideas that I used to bethump him with in the early nineties. What did I think would be the outcome of the war? In replying, I pointed out that when we had been duly punished for our national sins, we were as certain to win through as the sun was to rise. Israel was told that when they obeyed not God's commandments and God's laws they would be punished. And how would they be punished? With the stripes of men. By the Assyrian coming down on them like a wolf on the fold. The Assyrians took Israel captive starting in the year 741 B.C. and finishing in the year 676 B.C., thereby fulfilling what the prophet Isaiah had predicted,—that in seventy-five years Ephraim should be broken and not a people.

THE DESTINY OF AMERICA

They were scattered among the Assyrians across the Euphrates. At that time the Assyrians cut down Israel's vines and fruit trees, a thing forbidden in the Bible. Prussia is modern Assyria, and when the Huns retired to the Hindenburg line in the spring of 1917, they ran true to type. In the Bapaume sector they cut down every vine and fruit tree in every French garden for fifty miles, and many of these trees came out in bloom weeks later as they lay murdered on the ground. It was one of the saddest sights I saw at the Front. Wilfully to saw down fruit trees that were of no use to them or to us was fouling the usages of war. But Germany was out to maim France for life, and their poisoning wells and murdering fruit trees was a small item in the long list of barbarities and wilful premeditated destructions.

Though at the time of writing to my friend we had been driven back on Amiens and "had our backs to the wall," I wrote that when we had received our due punishment for our neglect to clean up Turkey for their slaughtering of the Armenians in Gladstone's time; for our neglect to fulfil our word to help Denmark when Germany stole Schleswig-Holstein from her; for our neglect to help France in 1870; for our other national sins; and for our neglect of God;—then we would win through because we are the everlasting kingdom, the Kingdom of Israel, spoken of by Jeremiah the prophet.

"For I am with thee [Israel], saith the Lord, to save thee: though I make a full end of all nations whither I have scattered thee, yet will I not make a full end of thee: but I will correct thee in measure, and will not leave thee altogether unpunished." (Jer. 30:11.)

I had promised my wife in June, 1918, to eat Christmas dinner, 1918, with her and the kiddies in Canada with the war all over, and I ventured the opinion to my friend that we would be likely to have Germany licked by August, 1918.

The newspapers of my home town published this opinion in June of 1918, because the real soldiers on the British staffs then said we were in for two more years war.

The mills of God grind slowly, but they grind exceeding sure. Doubtless Gladstone thought he was saving lives by not cleaning up the "Sick Man of Europe" when all Christendom cried out at the Armenian murders of that day. But what was the direct result of his saving the Turks? The hundreds of thousands of British and their Allies killed and wounded at Kut, Gallipoli, etc., by Turkey. If Britain had performed her national duty then, there would have been no vigorous Turkey to assist Germany in 1914. What did it cost Britain for this national political weakness in wounded, in lives lost, and treasure spent during those five awful years of carnage in Europe's cockpit—Flanders and Northern France? If Germany had not been allowed to take Schleswig-Holstein and had not been given Heligoland (given to Britain by the Creator as a waste place), there would have been no Kiel Canal; and if, in addition, Germany had not been allowed to overrun France in 1870, this last war would have been finished in perhaps six months or a year. I believe it pays nations as well as business men to do the right thing at the right time.

God gave Israel a world commission down through the ages, to break every yoke and lift every burden. But the American or United States section of Israel broke this law of God by placing yokes on negro men and women and making them slaves. With what result? Did they get away with it? For a time, just as Britain did with saving Turkey; but the mills of God were grinding out His judgment on this section of His chosen people, and that wrong had to be righted. How? Again by the stripes of men, South against North, and your President Lincoln finally said, "Slavery must be and will be abolished and these United States will not be divided in twain, half slave and half free."

When the tribe of Manasseh, U.S.A., were in Canaan, they were in two parts, as divided by Joshua: east of the Jordan and west of the Jordan. It is co-incident that, when they were in

America, 2,500 years later, the Dixie line divided them again into two parts, North and South.

God raised up Moses to unite and lead the united states or tribes of Israel out of bondage in Egypt. So, I believe, did he raise up Abraham Lincoln, Man of God, born of Puritan stock from Britain, the great leader of Manasseh, the United States of America—that "great people" the prophets had predicted they were to become. With what wise and farseeing judgment did Lincoln work towards unity, to win the war and establish peace!

Read John Wesley Hill's *Abraham Lincoln Man of God,* with Forewards by Major-General Leonard Wood, David Lloyd George, and President Warren G. Harding, if you desire to know how like Moses he was in leading the American children of Israel through their trials and tribulations toward peace and unity.

Lincoln quotations herein are all taken from Mr. Hill's book. If ever a man placed reliance on God for actual everyday performance right on American soil, in answer to prayer, that man was your martyred President, Abraham Lincoln. Lincoln believed that God answered prayer for America; and after the bitter disappointments and agonies of the dark days of 1863, after Fredericksburg had fallen, when treason stalked through the land, he issued the following proclamation, March 30, 1863:

"Whereas, The Senate of the United States, devoutly recognizing the supreme authority and just government of Almighty God in all the affairs of men and nations, has by a resolution requested the President to designate and set apart a day for National prayer and humiliation, and whereas, it is the duty of Nations as well as of men to own their dependence upon the overruling power of God, to confess their sins and transgression in humble sorrow, yet with assured hope that genuine repentence will lead to mercy and pardon, and to recognize the sublime truth announced in the Holy Scriptures and proven by all history, 'That those Nations only are blessed whose God is the Lord.'

"And, inasmuch as we know that by His divine law nations, like individuals, are subjected to punishments, and chastisements in this world, may we not justly fear that the awful calamity of civil war which now desolates the land may be but a punishment inflicted upon us for our presumptious sins to the needful end of our National reformation as a whole people!

"We have been the recipients of the choicest bounties of heaven; we have been preserved these many years in peace and prosperity; we have grown in number, wealth, and power as no other Nation has ever grown. But we have forgotten God.

"We have forgotten the gracious hand which preserved us in peace and multiplied and enriched and strengthened us, and we have vainly imagined, in the deceitfulness of our hearts, that all these blessings were produced by some superior wisdom and virtue of our own. Intoxicated with unbroken success we have become too self-sufficient to feel the necessity of *redeeming and preserving grace,* too proud to pray to the God who made us. It behooves us, then, to humble ourselves before the offended power, to confess our National sins, and to pray for clemency and forgiveness.

"Now, therefore, in compliance with the request, and *fully concurring in the views* of the Senate, I do by this my proclamation designate and set apart Thursday the 30th day of April, 1863, as a day of National humiliation, to abstain on that day from their ordinary secular pursuits, and to unite in their several places of public worship and devoted to the humble discharge of the religious duties proper to that solemn occasion.

"All this being done in sincerity and truth let us then rest humbly in the hope authorized by the divine teachings, that the united cry of the Nation will be heard on high and answered with blessings no less than the pardon of our National sins and the restoration of our now divided and suffering country to its former happy condition of unity and peace."

These prayers of a nation and of its President were answered as were also the prayers of General George Washington for his people and his army in 1776-1799.* And Lincoln took many many occasions to unite the nation in thanksgiving to the Almighty for the success the Almighty brought to their arms.

May 9, 1864, when General Grant was pounding Lee's army with artillery and infantry

---

*Read *George Washington, the Christian,* by William J. Johnson and see how absolutely this Father of his Country depended upon prayer to the mighty God of Battles during those trying times at Valley Forge. See his prayer on page 33: "Holy and eternal Lord God who art the King of Heaven and the *Watchman of Israel that never slumbereth or sleepeth,* What shall we render unto thee for all thy benefits? because thou hast inclined thine ears unto me therefore will I call on thee as long as I live."

attacks and following the bloody battles of the Wilderness, Lincoln issued the following:

> "To the friends of Union and Liberty: Enough is known of army operations within the last five days, to claim a special gratitude to God, while what remains undone demands our most sincere prayer to and reliance upon Him, without Whom all our efforts is in vain. I recommend that all patriots at their homes, in their place of public worship, and wherever they may be, unite in common thanksgiving and prayer to Almighty God."

Lincoln fully believed that our Creator was keeping watch over the Republic and Lincoln was right; God had promised His nation Israel that He would be with them wherever they went and when they sought Him, they would surely find Him. "Yielding and accommodating in nonessentials he was inflexibly firm on a principle or position deliberately taken."

"Let us have faith that Right makes Might," he said, "and in that faith let us to the end dare to do our duty as we understand it."

Lincoln was called to see that God's law was carried out in the country selected by the Creator for the thirteenth tribe of Israel (Manasseh) to inhabit. He strove to bring unity and law—to make God's law, and His command to break every yoke and lift every burden, the law of America from the northernmost point in the North to the southern end of the South.

What did it cost America for not knowing their identity and God's plan for running this new world, of which we are the heirs? The *Encyclopedia Britannica* puts the Union losses in killed at 359,528 men, the losses of the South as many, and in addition over 280,000 in the North and South died in a few years as a result of wounds, hardships, etc. That is, roughly, one million of your finest men killed, and by 1879, it had cost your Government in cash, including pensions, $6,190,000,000. "Who is blind, but my servant [Israel]?"

Where is the financier to-day who would think that America's investment in slaves turned out to be a paying proposition? Yet, Americans to-day are making similar investments that will all have to be paid for by the lives of your choicest men and by billions of money, because you are blind to your identity and to the Creator's plan for your national guidance; and, as a nation, your elected representatives are breaking God's divine commands, and your children and mine will pay in full measure for your neglect and my neglect for not seeing that our representatives carry out the Creator's commission, given to His people Israel, for *we* Celto-Saxons are Israel plus all believers who accept Christ and so are grafted into Israel's vine.

When I see some of your enthusiastic people who so firmly believe in the League of

Nations as a guarantee against war, I turn me to the greatest history (His-story, God's story) of the greatest people the world has ever possessed, the Bible, and I find "Armageddon" is yet to be fought; and ere it is fought, comes a time of trouble, such a time of trouble as the world has never seen before nor ever will see, "the time of Jacob's trouble"—and we Canadians, Yanks and British are all of Jacob's seed. But at the end we shall finally be saved out of it.

The allwise Creator laid down His plan through the mouths of His prophets and later through His son, our Lord, for the handling of all world problems by His executive nation Israel, of which the church was a part. "Thou, Israel art my servant." "With thee will I break in pieces the nations." Did the church ever smash nations? Yet ministers claim the church is Israel! "He cast out the heathen also before them." "I will subdue thine enemies." "They that strive with thee shall perish." Also "Be ye not unequally yoked together."

Then after we won the war, along comes our politicians and yours at Versailles; and instead of taking the allwise Creator's plan for peace and world progress as their basis, without publicly, at any rate, asking guidance of God through prayer, such as George Washington and Abraham Lincoln always asked for and received, these men start in without any public recognition of the almighty Creator, Ruler, and Upholder of this universe of His and presume to lay down laws and rules to guide God's world to peace and prosperity—and look at the results to-day! Many of the best people among all nations approve: but, gentlemen, it is foredoomed to failure. "Be ye not unequally yoked together" is as applicable to-day as the first day that it was spoken. "Say ye not, A confederacy, to all them to whom this people shall say, A confederacy; neither fear ye their fear, nor be afraid. Sanctify the Lord of hosts Himself; and let Him be your fear." (Isa. 8:12, 13.)

The men who think that they can yoke together forty—or is it forty-five divergent outfits?—with ideals as opposite as the north pole is from the south, and that this aggregation can work justly and bring in peace and righteousness when the workers of iniquity get among them have got another think or two coming their way ere they see daylight and peace.

The allwise Creator, who saw the end from the beginning, laid down an entirely different plan, which, when acknowledged and accepted by Britain, America, and their offspring, will cause a league of the Anglo-Saxon-Celtic nations the world over, and they, having the same language, ideas, and ideals of justice and truth, and being God's chosen company or commonwealth of nations, will bring about what the Creator has ordained from the beginning—righteous peace. But first Armageddon will have to be fought and won, and America will in that day fight side by side with their brother, Ephraim of the Isles, John Bull, and the other Anglo-Saxon nations from the uttermost parts of the earth. India, Arabia, and Japan will be with us and again we will win, as we did the last war, through divine help. Then and not till then can the Armstrongs, the Vickers Co., the Krupps, the United States Steel Corporation, and all the other armament makers the world over scrap their armament departments, because war will be over and done with for a thousand years and, in the ordinary course of events, if my reckoning is correct, a Charles M. Schwab will be on hand to do his scrapping for his company. Perhaps he may take advantage of this advance information and get his plans matured and ready for the coming change. Stranger things have happened.

When the world is in the melting pot, what is it worth in dollars and cents, and even in the depreciated pounds, shillings and pence, to know what is on the cards for the future of Britain and America.

Well, it is all to be had in the cheapest book published in the world, our Bible, and this screed is written for the purpose of giving you a key to "God's living Word" which has become almost a dead word in the nominal Christian of to-day, because unenlightened ministers of the Gospel have switched us on to a siding with a dead end, though our ticket calls for a Pullman on the fastest train operating on the main lines of the continental through express.

We think highly of a stockbroker who can foresee the turn of the market a few days or weeks ahead, in time to let us in or out, as we happen to want. What should we think of one who over 2500 years ago foretold that Ephraim, Israel (the English) would "do in" Turkey, or Edom, as she did in 1917 just at the end of the predicted 1335 lunar years of the Turkish calendar (and so ended the desolation standing in the Holy Place—see Daniel 12); who foretold that Judah and Israel would again possess their possessions in the Holy Land which extends from the river Nile to the Euphrates; and who foretold the earlier taking of the Ten Lost Tribes captive by the Assyrians, and later the scattering and *sifting of them among all the nations yet not a grain of the seed should be lost*. Ezekiel said:

"Thus saith the Lord God; Although I have cast them [Israel] far off among the heathen, and although I have scattered them among the countries yet will I be to them as a little sanctuary in the countries where they shall come." (Ezek. 11:16.)

This statement could not refer to the Kingdom of Judah (the Jews). They were not carried captive by Nebuchadnezzar, nor was Jerusalem destroyed until seven years after this prediction was made, so that it must refer to the northern kingdom of Israel, the Ten Tribes that had been carried captive by Assyria 123 years previously.

God has been "as a sanctuary" to all peoples who have gathered into the British Isles from 1600 B.C. From this gathering together in the "isles of the west" one branch was to break away (U.S.A.), because the way was too strait and they must have more freedom to practice their religion in the way they desired, and breaking away, they were to become a great people who, with Mother Britain, were to be a blessing to all nations of the earth.

"The children which thou [Israel] shalt have, after thou hast lost the other [the U.S.A. breaking away], shall say in thine ears, The place is too strait [too small] for me: give place to me that I may dwell." (Isa. 49:20.) And from Mother Britain then started those people who built up these wonderful young nations, Canada, Australia, New Zealand, Newfoundland, South Africa, etc.

The time of treading down the Holy Places in Palestine by the Turk having ceased, the time of the Gentiles is finished and we can tell just how far along we are and can estimate when, according to the prophets, the other trials due us are coming, and when that awful day of God Almighty, "Armageddon", is to come, wherein Israel is specifically warned: "Prepare ye for battle." As yet our politicians and leaders and, I am sorry to say, our preachers are blind as bats towards this most essential leadership of the prophetic teachings confirmed by Jesus when he was on earth, for our guidance.

> "Jerusalem shall be trodden down of the Gentiles [how long?], until the times of the Gentiles be fulfilled." (Luke 21:24.)
> "Blindness in part is happened to Israel [for how long?], until the fulness of the Gentiles be come in." (Rom. 11:25.)

Well, Jerusalem having ceased to be trodden down by the Turk (Gentiles), the time is now ripe for the Americans to cease their blindness towards this most essential question for your national guidance. In other words, get on to your job! See who you are, and act according to God's plans and specifications.

Most religious teachers are strong on data for the next world, quite overlooking the fact that two-thirds of the Old Testament and much of the New deals with prophecies and instructions for Israel, to be used and fulfilled in this everyday old world of ours here and now, where God's Kingdom is and has been during the last three thousand years. When Jesus was on earth, he said, "I am not sent but unto the lost sheep of the house of Israel." (Matt. 15:24.) If the Father of all sent Christ "but unto the lost sheep of the house of Israel," as our Lord told the people He did, it would seem rather important that our spiritual leaders and parsons should get a hump on and hasten to find these select but lost people, because no man, I care not how high he be in church or state, can properly interpret the Bible unless he can locate the nation Israel (as distinct from Judah), with which two-thirds of the Bible deals; and don't forget that Israel, God's chosen Hebrew people, are mentioned in prophetic dispatches some 2,543 times, so can readily be traced and found. Jesus said (Matt. 5:17): "Think not that I am come to destroy the law, or the prophets: I am not come to destroy, but to fulfill."

Now, here are all those prophecies concerning the nation Israel with David's seed ruling during the "Latter Days" when Jerusalem should cease to be trodden down by the Gentiles and be captured and restored to the Jews by Israel. What have our blind teachers of God's Word to say that will help us find the way laid down for both the United States and the British sections of Israel to follow in these troublous times?

Jesus in Luke 19, when questioned by his followers whether the Kingdom of God should immediately appear, referring to his own mission on earth at that date said: "A certain nobleman went into a far country to receive for himself a kingdom, and to return. And he called his ten servants [note the number] and delivered them ten pounds, and said unto them, Occupy [my kingdom] until I come. But his citizens [the Jews of Judah] hated him, and sent a message after him, saying: We will not have this man to *reign over us.''* You will see in verse 27 what becomes of these Jews who refuse to have him reign over them.

In Isaiah, Chapter 41, verse 8, Israel is specifically branded as *"my servant."* "But thou, Israel, art my servant... Thou whom I have taken from the ends of earth, and called thee from the chief men thereof, and said unto thee, *Thou art my servant; I have chosen thee.''*

You will note that Jesus did not hand his "kingdom" over to the churches as the churches' number throughout both Old and New Testaments is seven. Neither did he hand it to the disciples because they were twelve in number. But he did hand it over to the ten-tribed House of Israel, his ten servants, and commissioned them to *occupy his kingdom,* over which the enduring throne of David was to rule until He should again come whose right it is as King of Kings and ruler of Israel.

When Jesus was arranging for the future, what commission did he give to his disciples? "Go not into the way of the Gentiles, and into any city of the Samaritans enter ye not: but go rather to the lost sheep of the house of Israel,'' he said. One is safe in saying that our Lord knew the Hebrew Bible inside out and God's plan for Israel down through the ages; hence he sent his chosen workmen, the disciples, to preach to those "lost sheep" first, that, having converted them, they would be his instruments for bringing God's light, law, and justice to the whole world, as was predicted in the prophecies which he said he came to fulfill.

Ask your parson to-day: where is Israel, God's chosen people who were to be not the least but the chiefest of nations on earth? And the chances are 990 to 1,000 that you'll have him up a tree. He'll likely say they are the Jews, though they are as much Jews as a Scotchman is an Englishman; an Englishman an Irishman; or as an American is an Icelander, and no more, as I will prove to you further on.

Ezekiel, after condemning the shepherds, preachers and leaders of Israel (the Anglo-Saxon nations) says:

> "I will require my flock at their hand, and cause them [the shepherds] to cease from feeding the flock . . . For thus saith the Lord God; Behold, I, even I, will both search my sheep, and seek them out. . . . And ye my flock, the flock of my pasture, *are men,* and *I am your God,* saith the Lord God." (Ezek. 34:10, 11, 31.)

What an indictment against the ministers of America, Canada, Britain, Australia, New Zealand, and the others, for their failure to seek

God's chosen nation, Israel, His ten chosen servants, the Ten Lost Tribes, God's "lost sheep," His "flock"!—and "the flock" of His "pasture" are *men*. The tribe of Judah or the Jews have never been lost because "the shew of their countenance doth witness against them" down through the ages just as foretold (Isa. 3:9). Our negligent parsons will pay the price for their neglect to search the Scriptures on this point as commanded by God, and the Almighty will take over their job of finding and making Israel known to all the world without the aid of the shepherds.

If there is any doubt that the laws, commands and prophecies for national Israel, wherever they are, are still in force, look at the last chapter in the Old Testament, Malachi 4:4, wherein we are specifically ordered to remember "the law of Moses, my servant, which I commanded unto him in Horeb [for whom?] for all Israel, with the statutes and judgments."

Well, what is the use of the command, the last commandment in the Old Testament, if our neglectful ministers fail to locate where "all Israel" are to-day to whom this applies?

"And he [Elijah] shall turn the heart of the fathers to the children, and the heart of the children to their fathers, lest I come and smite the earth with a curse." (Mal. 4:6.)

What does this last statement in the Old Testament mean? If we are Israel—and we are

—then Abraham, Isaac, and Jacob were our fathers, and we are their children, and our hearts are to be turned towards them so that we may see and believe it lest we be smitten with a curse for neglecting to find God's Israel, His executive nation with His enduring, ruling dynasty promised in Psalms 89.

DETAILS OF CHAPTER II.

1. When Jeremiah went to Ireland with "God's house" and throne.
2. Our Israelite forefathers were ordered to set up waymarks and they did.
3. The Cradle of the Anglo-Saxons.
   Isaac-sons in Crimea.
4. Ephraim Israel was to become a company or commonwealth of nations.
5. Israel's new name, Isaac-sons, "In Isaac shall thy seed be called."
6. The United States the first branch of Joseph to run over the wall.
7. Herbert Hoover, food controller, like his predecessor and our forefather Joseph in Egypt.
8. America's costly Egyptian waymark in New York City.
9. The brotherhood of Britain and United States started 1711 B.C.
10. 1882 Foretold as a wonderful year for Israel, and it was!
11. Egyptian portion of land promised Abraham won by Israel England and U.S.A. sections.
12. American section (of Israel) represented by four ships of war.
13. John Bull and Brother Jonathan restore order in Egypt.

THE DESTINY OF AMERICA

14. Why Gladstone broke his word about Egypt.
15. Like as U.S.A. helped Britain in Egypt, so John bull helped Admiral George Dewey at Manilla, providentially.
16. Why Britain got Suez and U.S.A. got Panma, both fulfilling Bible prophecy.
17. Why Anglo-Saxon-Celts are God's elect, for service to the world.
18. Brith-ain of the Isles. God's light to the Gentiles.
19. Admiral Lord Fisher says: "Let us thank God that we are the Lost Ten Tribes of Israel!"
20. Anglo-Saxons have the Hebrew laws, the Hebrew Bible, the Hebrew measurements, and had largely the Hebrew language.
21. Wm. Tyndall, the Bible translator, says the Hebrew tongue agreeth a thousand times more with the English than with the Latin.
22. "The church" is not Israel though she was to be "in Israel" just as Scotland is not Great Britain, though she is in Great Britain.

CHAPTER II.

The children of Israel, including the tribe of Manasseh (U.S.A.), were instructed in many things by the prophet Jeremiah who, according to Jeremiah 1:10, Ferrar Fenton's version, says:

> "See! I have appointed you to-day over nations, and kingdoms; to pull up, and to break down, and to destroy, and to erase; as well as to build, and to plant."

Jeremiah was born 675 B.C., so he witnessed the pulling up, breaking down, and erasing of the kingdom of Judah, the killing of the king's son, and taking prisoners of the remnant of the nation. About 581 B.C. Jeremiah started on the latter part of his divine commission of building and planting. Accompanied by the royal seed, Zedekiah's daughter, Tamar Tephi, and Baruch, his scribe, he started for Ireland. Ten different Irish histories record the fact that at this time a wonderful prophet arrived in Ireland who caused Baal worship to cease, married his ward (Zedekiah's daughter) to the then ruling king of Ireland, who also was of the seed of David through the Zarah branch, on condition that the king should found a school for prophets.

THE DESTINY OF AMERICA

This was built at Tara and for five hundred years the educated men of Europe came to Ireland to absorb wisdom and learning from this school founded by Jeremiah, and to-day in the Court of Justice in Dublin, in the position of honor, is the medallion of Jeremiah cut in enduring stone as a waymark of his former presence there.

See Jeremiah 31:21 where Israel was instructed to set up waymarks:

> "Set thee up waymarks, make thee high heaps: set thine heart toward the highway, even the way which thou wentest."

You will naturally wonder whether Israel carried out these instructions, and for your information I can advise that they did. So, Israel's wanderings can be traced from the very place where they were taken as captives by the Assyrian king, Shalmaneser, that is, to the southwest of the Caspian Sea.

Diodorus writes: The Sacae sprung from a people in Media.

Ptolemy found the Saxons in a race of Sythians called Sakai who came from Media.

Pliny says: The Sakai were among the most distinguished people of Scythia, who settled in Armenia and were called Sacae-Sani.

Albinus says: "The Saxons were descended from the ancient Sacae in Asia."

Prideaux finds that the Cimbrians (Kumrii) came from between the Black and Caspian seas and with them came the Angli.

Plutarch, Tacitus, and Ptolemy show clearly that the Anglo-Saxons, the Sacae and the Scythians and the Getae were the same people.*

While this place became the national grave of rebellious Israel, wonderful as it may seem, it is no less the cradle of the Anglo-Saxon-Celtic race, as traced by the historian, Sharon Turner, 120 years ago and more recently by Major B. de W. Weldon in *The Evolution of Israel,* and also in his later work, *The Origin of the English.*

These people, having been separated from God on account of their sins, were not to be known or recognized as God's people until they should repent of their sins and accept Christ's message to the lost sheep of Israel; but it was foretold in Genesis 21:12, "In Isaac shall thy seed be called." The tribes broke up into sections and wandered under various names, as Scythians, Goths, Gatae, the largest mass or body of Gatae being called "Massagatae," and under the divine impulse to push westward they trekked north of the Black Sea into the Crimea. They started out calling themselves *Isaac-sons;* and there are many tombstones in the Crimea bearing names and dates stating that the dead are Isaac-sons and children of captivity, and giving the very period of their

---

* *"God's Covenant Man,"* by E. Odlum, M.A., B.Sc., etc.

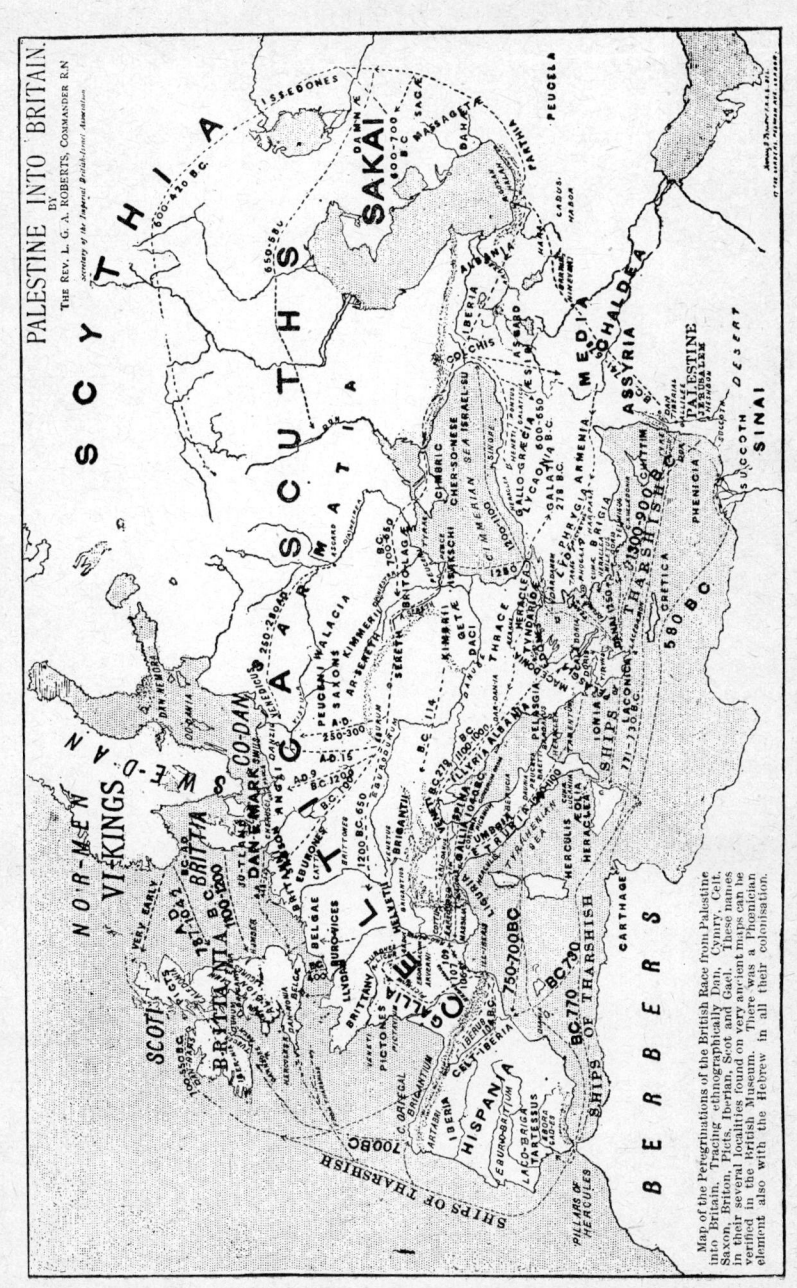

Map of the Peregrinations of the British Race from Palestine into Britain. Tracing ethnographically Dan, Cymry Celt, Saxon, Briton, Picts, Iberian, Scot and Gael. These names in their several localities found on very ancient maps can be verified in the British Museum. There was a Phoenician element also with the Hebrew in all their colonisation.

captivity and the commencement of the nation—when Israel came out of Egypt under Moses. There are no vowels in Hebrew so the *I* was not pronounced, and in time Isaac-sons got to be called *Saac-sons* and on their tombstones it is so written, and it is now spelled Saxons. *Engle* in Hebrew is bull, and the bull tribe of Isaac-sons were called *Engle* or *Angle-Saxons,* as the centuries rolled on. Everywhere these Saac-sons went, they left waymarks* until they took up their abode in the isles of the sea north and west from Palestine, where the prophets foretold God would appoint a place for them, where they would be moved no more; where they would have rest; and where their enemies would not be able to afflict them, as in former times, so that they could grow strong and become "a great nation" as prophesied in Genesis 12:2, 3:

> "And I will make of thee a great nation, and I will bless thee, and make thy name great; and thou shalt be a blessing: and I will bless them that bless thee, and curse him that curseth thee: and in thee shall all families of the earth be blessed."

No other nation has ever had the word "great" as part of their national name. Why? This could not apply to the Jews because they have never been a blessing where they went and they never will be until they realize that the

---

*See Major B. deW. Weldon's *The Evolution of Israel, the Story of the English Race from 721 B.C. to the Present Day.*

Anglo-Saxons are Israel and that all the blessings for Judah can only come through Israel as foretold in the Old Testament.

They were finally to become a company or "multitude of nations." (Gen. 48:19.) Great Britain certainly has become "a multitude [or commonwealth] of nations" with her Anglo-Saxon offspring, forming nations and colonies the world over, the first of her offspring being the United States of America.

See Genesis 49:22 to get a line on the inheritance surely belonging to Great Britain (Great Covenant Land) and the United States:

> "Joseph is a fruitful bough, even a fruitful bough by a well [or water]; whose branches run over the wall."

The United States branch ran over the wall when your Pilgrim Fathers, all Englishmen, beat it for America. The Australian branch beat it for the antipodes. The Canadian branch ran over the wall from Britain and also from the U. S. A., because when your citizens decided to do without a king as the head of your organization, many loyal Britishers of English, Scotch, and Irish brands left everything they possessed in the U. S. A. and took up their abode in the wooded wilderness of Canada rather than be disloyal to their King and Governor, who, imperfect though he proved to be, was still the instrument of God.

THE DESTINY OF AMERICA

They (the United Empire Loyalists who left the U. S. A.) were not of the Manasseh seed who were to become a great people, so they pulled out and have been the backbone of Canadianism ever since.

Other branches ran over the wall all over the world; and a right husky lot of branches or lion's cubs they proved themselves to be in France and Belgium, in Italy, in Gallipoli, in Mesapotamia, and in Egypt, fighting and holding the Hun while brother Jonathan was making ready his millions to send over to help.

To-day Canada, Australia, New Zealand, South Africa, Newfoundland, India, and the dozens of Colonies and possessions all are ruled by the offspring of British stock; all proudly hail George V. as their King and Governor, and he is as clearly descended from King David, King of Israel, as you are from your grandfather, as is proven by W. M. H. Milner's book, *The Royal House of Britain an Enduring Dynasty*.

> Gen. 49:23: The archers [or warriors] have sorely grieved him, and shot at him, and hated him [Joseph]:
> 24. But his bow abode in strength, and the arms of his [Joseph's] hands were made strong by the hands of the mighty God of Jacob; (from thence is the shepherd, the stone of Israel).

In Ferrar Fenton's version this last clause reads: "From Whom is Israel's guardian stone"

—that "guardian stone" which rests in Westminster Abbey and upon which kings and queens of the seed of David have been crowned since the prophet Jeremiah took it to Ireland about 579 B.C. Ferrar Fenton in his splendid translation of the Bible into modern English says (Jer. 31:21):

> "Set up your Beacons,—your Landmarks set up!
> Fix your hearts on the mounds by the way that
>   you marched.
> Return, Israel's daughter, return to your City."

"The tribe of Dan, whose homeland was Jordan (Jor-dan) and who stayed in their ships, were bold and enterprising. Their first camping ground they named Mahaneh-Dan and along their lines of travel we find the names they left behind them in the Dan-ube, the Dan-iester, the Dan-au, the Dan-an, the Dan-inn, Dan-tzig, Dan-etz, the Dan-aster, the Dan-dari, the Danez, the Don, the Dacia, the Sea of Moses and the Country of Moses or Morcia, the Dan-ric Alps, the Danish archipelago, etc. In Ptolemy's map of Ireland we find Dans-lough, Dan-Sower, Dan Sobairse, Dan's resting place and Dan's habitation and Dan-gan castle (the birthplace of the Duke of Wellington).

"The old inhabitants of Ireland were called Dan-onians and it is well known that among the ancient kings of Ireland there were several

Davids, three Solomons and a Daniel and Jeremiah in every house down to Daniel O'Connell and beyant."*

When Joseph, our first food controller, was keeping the Egyptians from starving during the seven lean years, 1700 B.C. to 1693 B.C. (as the U.S.A. through its servant and food controller, Herbert Hoover, helped the Belgians), his two sons—Manasseh, born 1711 B.C., and Ephraim, born 1712 B.C.—were doubtless playing around the public square and Temple of On in that large Egyptian City of Memphis, a few miles from where Cairo now stands, and in full view of that greatest wonder of the world the Great Pyramid of Gizeh, built by Shem in 2170 B.C. In that public square in front of the temple in Memphis stood two obelisks—and there are no other two in the world just like them. Where are those obelisks to-day? Does it seem strange that one of these obelisks, several thousand years later, should find its way from Egypt to America and should be set up in your largest city? This Egyptian obelisk, popularly called Cleopatra's Needle, is of rose-red Syene granite and was actually presented to the city of New York by Ismael, Khedive of Egypt, in 1877. I wonder why of all the nations on this round earth he happened to select America—what is your guess?

Fifty Reasons Why the Anglo-Saxons are Israelites, by W. H. Poole.

It was brought to New York in 1880 at the expense of $100,000 by Mr. W. H. Vanderbilt and was erected in Central Park in 1881, where it stands to-day, proudly rearing its pointed apex skyward as a waymark to all America of the place of origin of your forefather Manasseh, and the starting place of your world-wide wanderings since you left Egypt under Moses.

The children of Israel marched out of Egypt under Moses about 1492 B.C., and, if the U. S. A. section of Israel is representatively to "return to your city," it is rather important that you know the city that your progenitor came from, is it not? Well, your largest city has your waymark waiting since 1881 for Americans, both Jews and Israelites, to realize their identity; and waiting for them to take their full part in the world inhertance given to their forefathers, Abraham, Isaac, and Jacob, Joseph and Manasseh. See Genesis 48:4: "Behold, I will . . . give this land to thy seed after thee for an everlasting possession," and it has been in the possession of Abraham's seed ever since, as the Turk is descended from Esau, Jacob's brother.

The souls of most men and women who have given them a reasonable chance for expression and growth by following the wee small voice of Conscience or Spirit, as it moves us, know more than the same men or women can adequately voice or explain to outsiders. Likewise, the Soul of America knows more than its politicians, who have been led by a way they know not, to do the things God has laid out for the American section of Israel to bring about.

You will remember that the Holy Land, from the river Nile to the Euphrates in Mesopotamia, was promised to Israel, for an inheritance.

In this area lies the Suez Canal, built for the Khedive by that farseeing enterprising French engineer, de Lesseps, with French men, money and brains. But it was not for France to hold. You may remember that that farseeing son of Judah, Benjamin D'Israeli (or Benjamin of Israel) when the Khedive was hard up, bought a controlling interest in the canal for the Covenant Land (Brith-ain), for about £4,000,000 which had originally cost about £30,000,000; and so it passed to British ownership and control forever.

The Panama Canal, started by the same engineer, with French men, money, and machinery failed. But Israel was promised the waste place of the earth and the control of the sea and the rivers afar and the gates. So, after millions had been spent on it, the machinery rotted until the Manasseh tribe of Israel took it over; and then the gigantic task went digging to completion. So the two brother nations have not only a Cleopatra's Needle apiece to mark their origin,—here I am ahead of my story—but they each own a canal started by another nation's cash. These canals connecting the seas are ours, because Israel was given command of the sea and their right hand was to be in the rivers afar—and it is and will so continue. "God moves in a mysterious way his wonders to perform!"

The Promised Land will be the most fertile land in the world. When irrigated it will grow four crops per year, and strange to say, this section of land, I am told, has never been sold or deeded to anyone since it was promised to Israel. They did not obey God's laws and were as a consequence scattered among the Gentiles. You can buy land in England, Canada, United States, anywhere, and get title to it. Years ago several colonization schemes were proposed for Palestine but the sultans of Turkey, when it came to a showdown, would never sell this land or give a deed; it was to be held for Judah and Israel—God's chosen people—to return to. If you wish to locate your section of it, read the last half dozen chapters of Ezekiel, where the survey is laid down in thirteen longitudinal strips, almost like an American flag—and don't overlook Chapter 47, verse 13, where it says, "Joseph shall have two portions": one for Manasseh, the representative of the great people (U. S. A.), and the other for Ephraim, the nation and company of nations (Britain, Canada, New Zealand, South Africa, India, Australia, etc.). The brotherhood of

Britain and the United States is ordained down through the ages, despite the machinations of the Land Leaguers, Fenians, Clan Na Gael, Sinn Fein, Pro-Germans and other more secret and insidious foes, some of whom, before America became a nation, had been working nights and Sundays to ditch old Britain, that Mother of Free Parliaments and breeder of free peoples.

The year 1882 was foretold in the Bible as a wonderful year for Israel, also by Piazzi Smyth, F. R. S. E., F. R. A. S., Astronomer Royal for Scotland, in his work, *Our Inheritance in the Great Pyramid of Egypt,* published in 1865, the third edition in 1877, a copy of which lies before me. It was also foretold by H. Grattan Guinness, D.D., in 1878, in his illuminating work, *The Approaching End of the Age,* (a book that ran through thirteen editions) and by many other authors. As Manasseh (America) and that other tribe, Ephraim (England), both sons of Joseph, came from Egypt, they will naturally be interested in Egypt's future developments.

Jeremiah 33:14 says: "Behold us, the days come, saith the Lord, that I will perform that good thing which I have promised unto the house of Israel and to the house of Judah." What good thing? That He will restore Israel again, one of a city and two of a family, united in the land that He gave them. But first we have to get that land, haven't we? How are we to get possession of it?

In 1882 Great Britain and France sent their fleets to Alexandria, Egypt, by agreement, to bombard and take possession of it. Arrangements were made by both admirals to bombard together; but you will remember that the French admiral, without authority, beat it home to Toulon with his whole fleet, without firing a shot. Why, I wonder? Was it not because that land was for Israel and it was not on the cards that France should have any hand in it, or be mixed up with or have any legitimate claim upon that particular bit of land? According to the Bible, Joseph was to win back Palestine from Turkey; and she did in 1917, just in the year Daniel predicted, the 1335th lunar year dating from the Hegira. See Daniel 12:12: "Blessed is he that waiteth, and cometh to the thousand three hundred and five and thirty days"—all prophetic days being considered as years in the Bible as in Ezekiel 4:5.

Who do you suppose landed with the British and helped Brother John restore law and order in Alexandria after it was bombarded? Well, it was Brother Jonathan who was on the job despite your rulers' many decisions, before and since, not to mix up in European matters. Your fleet landed their marines with the British. The *British Army and Navy Gazette* of February 24, 1883, says in part, "Admiral Nicholson, U.S.N., rendered this country [England] most valuable service at a critical moment in landing Marines at Alexandria after the bombardment to assist Lord Alcester in restoring law and order."

The American vessels of war that were at Alexandria at the time were the following:

1. Lancaster—First class Sloop of War—Capt. Bancroft Gherardi.

2. Galena—Iron Clad S. S. Third rate—Commander O. A. Batcheller.

3. Nipsic—Gunboat fourth class—Commander H. B. Seeley.

4. Quinnebaug—Gunboat fourth class—Commander William Whitehead.

The squadron was in command of Rear Admiral J. W. A. Nicholson, U.S.A.—not a very formidable looking lot, but Providence had them on the spot just when they were surely wanted, as the French admiral got a brain wave to beat it home, and was cashiered, I am told, for not carrying out his government's instructions to bombard and take possession with the British. Still there are people who cannot see God ruling through His chosen instrument Israel, the Anglo-Saxon Celts!

Well, Gladstone didn't want Egypt, and he said from the floor of the House, "We are only in Egypt to settle this matter and then we shall leave." Man proposes, even a big man, but God disposes; and Gladstone had to break his word, as we didn't get out of Egypt, despite Gladstone's many promises and Lord Salisbury's after him, nor have we gone since, as Providence so far has overruled every attempt to scuttle from Egypt.

Lord Dufferin, one of the most able Governor-Generals Canada has ever had (1872-1878), made a speeh about that time to the Empire Club in which he said:

> "I believe the time is too late for England to seek to disinherit herself from that noble destiny which I firmly believe she has been *entrusted of Providence*. The same hidden hand which planted the tree of Constitutional Liberty within her borders, and which has called upon her to become the Mother of Parliaments, has sent forth her children to possess the waste places of the earth. That her design has been to turn such to a Paradise of plenty, those present can best testify. I believe that great as have been the changes of our day, our children are destined to see still more glorious accomplishments."

Lord Dufferin in the above only said—and almost in Biblical words—what the prophets had foretold three thousand years ago as Israel's future; and she and America are fulfilling it every day of the 365 in the year.

Providence was again on the job when Admiral George Dewey took Manilla from Spain and the German admiral threatened him. I suppose you remember that, just as Brother Jonathan had happened in Alexandria Harbour when wanted in 1882, John Bull happened with a fleet in

Manilla Bay at a most opportune time, and the British fleet steamed between the anchored German fleet and the American. The Hun admiral had tried to bluff Admiral Dewey; Brother John heard of it, and, to show Germany that blood was thicker than water, altered his ships so that the first shell fired towards the American fleet would be at the British fleet. 'Twas a real brotherly action and one that was thoroughly appreciated by Admiral Dewey and his officers and by the American nation.

Admiral George Dewey at Manilla and Admiral Nicholson, U.S.N., at Alexandria, in 1882, may not have known it, but the Creator of this world gave Israel (both the U.S.A. and British sections) "the gate" of their enemies. (Gen. 22:17.) Now there is, and always has been, only one element that is "the gate" to all Israel's enemies, and that is the sea; and by God's grace we have it. In Psalm 89:25, we read:

"I will set his hand also in the sea, and his right hand in the rivers."

Ferrar Fenton's version has verses 24-26 as follows:

"His assailants I cut from his face,
And all who hate him will defeat.
With him are My Mercy and Truth,
And I lift up his horn by My Power.
So I placed his left hand on the Sea,
And his right to the Rivers afar!"

Well, both sections of Israel have had their assailants cut off; and Britain and America have always defeated those who hate them and, thank God, always will, as the throne of David is the throne of Jehovah on earth which He has sworn He will protect until Christ comes again to Jerusalem, this time to reign over the whole House of Israel, and the whole world.

The Brith-annia or Covenant of the deep, or rule of the sea—for this is its Hebrew meaning—belongs as much to one of Joseph's sons as to the other and is America's God-given charter for her navy as it is for Britain's. Under Britain the whole world was free to use the sea until Germany started to smash civilization. Not knowing the Creator's plan, your President left your shores with his grip packed with demands and arguments—for what? "The freedom of the seas," this old cry of the German, the Hun and the Turk, as if the world had not had every freedom of the sea until Germany started to smash civilization and we used our God-given rule of it against her. This demand and that of "no indemnities, no annexation" wrought harm for your friend, France. Germany must not be asked to indemnify her wilful destructions, but France, who bled at every pore, saving your hide as well as her own, must *indemnify America for the shot and shell she used in saving it!* Will America indemnify France the million and a half lives lost using the shells that

THE DESTINY OF AMERICA

saved the world, not France alone, from destruction?

"America's soul is unsettled!" said Harvey O. Higgins. Thank God it is! or 'twere almost useless to have souls. The British admiral's action at Manilla Bay was heartily commended by Americans of both political parties with the exception of the Clan-na-Gael (or was it the Land Leaguers of that time?), our and your inveterate enemies—enemies in Canaan and enemies still. They have run true to form ever since Israel took the promised land.

However, 'tis not to worry or be downhearted, because the mills of God are as surely grinding out His judgment for the behind hedges and other murderers in Erin as when America placed yokes on the sons and daughters of Ham and expected to get away with it. "By their fruits ye shall know them" is still the divine command; and "Whatsoever a man soweth, that shall he also reap" still holds good in America as in Ireland. The crops sown for years past will within a few years be garnered and many people, churchmen and politicians, will be surprised at the overdue portion coming to their sections. The Irish of all classes and creeds will then get their due justice with ordered liberty and real peace with real Home Rule. Ireland was set apart by Jehovah for Israel, not for the Canaanites, Phoenicians, Fenians or Sinn Feiners, over 1600 years B.C. and has been occupied by them ever since—and who are the Sinn Feiners who can claim right and title to what God gave to His covenant people or who can change the Creator's design? They have had many tries for it, but they have always failed and always will. Good will and justice can secure what force never can in Brith-ain, even in the Irish section of it. The supremacy of the law, God's law, must come first. Ulster will, I think, show them how—to all men of good will.

In Chapter 41 the prophet, speaking to the Brith Colony of Israel, says, "Keep silence before me, O islands [What islands? Look up any map and see any islands that it could possibly apply to save the British Isles]; and let the people renew their strength." (vs. 1.) "Thou, Israel, art my servant, Jacob whom I have chosen, the seed of Abraham my friend." (vs. 8.) "I will make thee a new sharp threshing instrument having teeth" (vs. 15) and so on; all through the balance of Isaiah the inspired phophet describes in varying stages Israel as she has been, is now, or is to be, and Mother Brith-ain fits it clause after clause and no other nation has or ever will fulfil those prophecies.

"The isles shall wait for his law." "My servant, Israel." Who are the people of the "isles"? There are not many isles to pick from nor many peoples who wait for "His law". If the

British in India, in Egypt, in China, in every heathen nation are not God's servants, what nation is or ever has been? Gentlemen, the Brithish (Covenant men—*Brith* meaning covenant and *ish* meaning men) are God's "servant," they wait for His law and they are in the islands where God said His servant would be; they fill every single specification—and Americans are as much Covenant men as are their brothers of the British Isles who did not migrate to America with George Washington's forebears.

As that grand old fighting British admiral, Lord Fisher, who foresaw 1914—and built Britain's 1914 war fleet in anticipation of it, says in his *Memories,* page 223, "Jerusalem, the Capital of 'The Lost Ten Tribes of Israel' *whom we are without doubt,* for how otherwise could ever we have so prospered when we have had such idiots to guide us and rule us as those who gave up Heligoland, Tangier, Curacoa, Corfu, Delagoa Bay, Java, Sumatra, Minorca, etc., etc.? I have been at all the places named, so am able to state from the personal knowledge that only congenital idiots could have been guilty of such inconceivable folly as to surrender them and again I say, LET US THANK GOD THAT WE ARE THE LOST TEN TRIBES OF ISRAEL!" John Bull muddles and muddles, but he always muddles through, and goodness knows that any other nation with a like capacity for muddling would have been on the scrap heap ages ago, but for the divine ruling.

Admiral Lord Fisher was a staunch Bible student as are so many leading soldiers and sailors of Britain. Just before his death when about to be operated upon, he asked his closest friend to be with him and if he saw that he was passing out, to whisper in his ear as he was crossing the bar, the following verse, "O Lord, in thee have I trusted, let me never be confounded." He confounded many enemies of Britain and spent his days and nights working with might and main to protect God's Kingdom and its enduring throne upon which sits the seed of David.

I was pleased indeed when the pastor of the church I attended in Canada held a memorial service in honor of this great servant in Israel.

What does British history say about "The isles shall wait for his law"? Well, Alfred the Great placed Israel's Hebrew laws (Moses' Ten Commandments and much of Deuteronomy) at the head of the laws of Britain in his time; and the laws of Britain, the United States and all the other Anglo-Saxon nations are based upon the Hebrew laws of Moses, every man being equal before the law—justice to all, rich and poor alike. Is it not strange that we Anglo-Saxons should adopt Hebrew laws for our own if we are not their descendants, national Israel?

THE DESTINY OF AMERICA

The Creator of this world certainly called Israel to be His servant, and God certainly has been with Britain and her offspring in all times of trouble; and the Anglo-Saxon-Celts have been a light to the Gentiles, doing His missionary work among the heathen to the ends of the earth, by means of foreign missionary societies and the churches for centuries, and added to recently by that grand Army with its Salvation banner floating among the heathen of all nations.

If Britain and her offspring are filling every item of the thousands of promises God made to and for Israel in the Bible, then gentlemen, I submit that we Anglo-Saxon-Celts must be Israel. These historical facts cannot be dodged, ducked or ignorantly set aside by business men in the troublous times we are yet to go through. "Ye shall know the truth and the truth shall make you free."

When America's business men understand the plan laid down for them by the Creator in the Bible (and I defy anyone to read intelligently one half the Bible unless they can locate the Hebrew nation of Israel, as well as Judah), then will America and Britain, and the Anglo-Saxon peoples, and the Jews the world round, have a compass and a chart by which they can direct their national and business sailings with absolute knowledge that they are working according to the divine plan; and then "God will prosper their undertakings" as the motto on America's Great Seal—*Annuit Coeptis*—proclaims.

It is interesting to remember that the Creator's chosen people were Hebrews and their writings were mostly in Hebrew. In the early days they divided peoples into two categories:

(1) Hebrews, or God's people.

(2) Heathen, all who were not Hebrews.*

It is also interesting to find the early inhabitants of the British Isles in Ireland, in Wales and in Scotland using the Hebrew language and forty per cent. of the English language based upon the Hebrew. Furthermore, we have used Hebrew weights and measures for 3,000 years, and they check with those found in the Pyramid built about 2170 B.C. by Shem, son of Noah,—though our yard stick is the one thousandth part shorter, perhaps due to wear and tear through the ages!

William Tyndall, who translated the New Testament, says, "The Greek agreeth more with the Englyshe than with the Latyne and the properties of the Hebrew tongue agreeth a thousand times more with the Englyshe than with the Latyne."

"My lore has been declared in Hebrew—in the Hebraic tongue," asserted Taliesin, the king or prince of Druid bards.

---

*See *The Kingdom of God,* by C. W. Eakeley—a gem of a book.

Dozens of other authorities could be quoted, but Tyndall settles the matter as far as my judgment is concerned.

The Hebrew word *Goyim* means nations though we have been so long taught by those who should know and do not (see Matt. 15:14) that it means "Gentiles" that most people accept it without question.

The Archbishop of Canterbury, I am told, in his sermon at the National Prayer Meeting for help during the war stated that Britain was a Gentile nation and he laid stress upon this false rendering.

It would upset the false teachings of the Episcopal Churchmen (with the accent on the men) of Britain if that section of the Church Universal were to see that, though Israel was to be scattered among the "nations," the Gentiles or heathen, it was to be but a temporary dispersion. But the prophets who predicted this scattering of Israel also said that Israel would be "sifted" among the nations, "like as corn is sifted" and that not a "grain" would be lost and he that scattered Israel would gather them. They were to have a place appointed unto them—in the Isles north and west from Palestine where they would move no more and where they would be strengthened and would become a nation, a great nation ("and thy name shall be great") and a "company" or "multitude of nations," from which one section was to break away and become a "great people," and they were to be God's people and eventually a nation of priests to God.

I would like to have the Archbishop of Canterbury's rendering of Genesis 17: 4, which reads, "As for me, behold, my covenant is with thee [Abraham], and thou shalt be a father of many nations [*Goyim*]. Surely God did not tell Abraham that he was to be a father of many heathen unbelievers or Gentiles but that He intended him to be the father of many nations who were, as promised to Israel, to inherit the earth,— as the Gentiles never will.

I may be wrong but it has always seemed to me that it is as necessary to use common sense in dealing with the Bible as it is in the army, which was rarely overloaded with that commodity, so necessary in business.

The church was to be *in* Israel but it could not *be* Israel because she in no sense fills the specifications laid down in hundreds of cases in the Bible that describe national, literal Israel, God's Hebrew people, His ten servants, His battle axe and weapons of war.

What is known as horse sense, with or without overmuch learning, is a great asset to most people, though the German "high lights" showed little of it when they signed that appeal to the world at the beginning of the war; and some of our Oxford variety exhibited a like amount after the war when they hankered to resume old relations before German professors or Germany had shown one single sign of repentance: "There are none so blind as those who will not see"—university professors included!

CHAPTER III.

1. Ephraim (England) was to become a Multitude or Commonwealth of Nations.
2. Why the Submarines and Zepps had to fail.
3. Why I didn't join the cavalry.
4. The Archbishop of Canterbury's visit to our Army.
5. The reason the Church of England languishes.
6. Outpouring of the Spirit due when they see this Truth.
7. Britain's totem pole from Egypt on the Thames embankment.
8. Why it did not sink in Biscay Bay when lost.
9. A wayside drink in Northern France.
10. Does Owen Wister understand America's destiny?
11. Manasseh Israel (U.S.A.) was to help establish the earth.
12. Your Pilgrim Fathers understood and appreciated this fact.
13. America's first name is "FORGETFULNESS," i.e. Manasseh.
14. The Pyramid on your Great Seal of State to locate where your forefather Joseph came from.
15. America and Britain possess all the Irsaelitish heraldry.

16. Armageddon yet to be fought, the "Great Day of God Almighty."
17. General Leonard Wood on America's unpreparedness.
18. Germany invented the poison gas of higher criticism.
19. If Brothers John and Jonathan can be divided, Germany still hopes to dominate the world.
20. *Thirteen* is America's national heraldic number.

CHAPTER III.

Now, what became of Manasseh's younger brother, Ephraim? Jacob, Joseph's father, when blessing Ephraim in Egypt, said: "His seed shall become a multitude of nations." (Gen. 48:19.) Ferrar Fenton's version has it in verses 19 and 20: "But his father refused, saying, 'I knew it my son, I knew it. He also [Manasseh] shall be a nation,—and he also shall be great,—but nevertheless his younger brother [Ephraim, England] shall be greater than he [Manasseh], and his race shall be a multitude [or commonwealth] of nations, and when blessing in that period they shall say, "The Blessing of Israel be upon you! May God make you like Ephraim and like Manasseh," and they will place Ephraim above Manasseh.'"

These two boys were brothers, and the nations springing from them are still and always will be called Brother Jonathan and Brother John or John Bull. One has grown into a great nation, just as predicted about the year 1689 B.C., and the other has grown into a multitude, or as some prophets state, "a company of nations," and the headquarters are located in the "isles of the sea," north and west of Palestine, where the prophets of old said Jehovah would select a place, a sanctuary for them, and where the other nations would afflict them no more, *as heretofore,* and they never have. Just note those saving words—"as heretofore."

When Israel was on the Continent among the nations, they were subject to invasion by Egyptian, Assyrian, African, Babylonian and Roman Empire troops, but when they beat it aross the English Channel, their island home would be inviolate and they could not be invaded in that manner any more. The Creator took care that the Spanish Armada and other attempted invasions were properly attended to by the elements when their enemies sought to subdue Britain. In like manner Providence has taken care of Old Mother Britain down through the ages, just as the children of Israel were to be taken care of by God that they might carry on His work. They have done it imperfectly, of course, but they have been about as perfect as are you and I and the other chaps making up these nations. But when we get wise as to who we are, what we are, and why we are, we will brush up our imperfections. Just read the 54th chapter of Isaiah and note the last verse:

"No weapon that is formed against thee [Israel] shall prosper; and every tongue that shall rise against thee in judgment thou shalt condemn. This is the heritage of the servants of the Lord, and their righteousness is of me, saith the Lord."

Could this possibly have been spoken about the Jews, who have never been servants of the Lord. "Their righteousness is of Me." They crucified our Lord and to-day they are still at the game prohibiting the word *Christian* from being even used in the free for all schools of America and will not even let Christmas carols be sung or Christmas trees be used in schools where they have power to kick them out. See Jewish activities in U. S. A. by Henry Ford's paper, *The Dearborn Independent,* Dearborn, Mich. Price 25 cents.

If we only realized that this heritage was for us Anglo-Saxon Celts, what a change for the better would come over the face of this earth! That prediction was comforting during the trying times when the Huns were raiding Britain with Zeppelins and raiding the seven seas with their submarines, manned by the most sinister pirates ever afloat, under instructions to "leave not a trace"—their record of sinking the Lusitania and hospital ships, etc., will remain an outstanding infamy so long as men exist.

Banking upon these prophecies meaning what they said, I was quite certain over our prospects of doing them in ere they put us out of commission with either Zepps or submarines.

I remember going into our mess late one morning when the only occupant was our senior parson, a charming Englishman and preacher

THE DESTINY OF AMERICA

(now a real live Bishop in gaiters). He was shaking his head and looking very glum as he perused the *Times* report of our last week's shipping sinkages.

"Many ships gone last week, Colonel?" I asked.

"I am afraid the Hun will do us in at the rate they are sinking our ships," he replied.

Then I quoted: "No weapon that is formed against thee [Israel] shall prosper"; but the Colonel being one of those knowledgeable higher critic chaps from Oxford, who, together with the German higher critics, have spiritualized away all God's enduring promises from "the latter" and other days, naturally could not see my cheerful outlook for a minute, and admitted that he could not read my "stuff" meaning a book of Marr Murray's on British-Israelism that I had loaned him (hoping to have an argument on the facts contained therein), but he ducked the issue by not reading it, alas!

My progenitors, when passing out tempers, cut mine a trifle short (the way I cut my hair), and I remember we finished the session by my remarking that if I knew as damn little about road-building as he did about prophecy and the Bible generally, I'd quit my road job and sign on with the cavalry (who at that time were mostly eating their heads off in the back areas and had been for years).

If these lines ever reach the Bishop I'm sure he will chuckle over some of the strenuous arguments we used to engage in: because, despite my many shortcomings, perhaps because of them, he seemed to have a liking for me; but, being an Englishman, he couldn't express it, though he presented me at different times with autographed copies of books he had written and when the Archbishop of Canterbury came to our Army Headquarters, I was among those who were invited to meet him, to give "a frank expression of our views on subjects of Church Reform, etc."

I've always regretted missing that "show," but after much wangling I had just succeeded in securing two weeks' leave to visit our Army of Occupation in Germany; and, having worked night and day for several years headed for the Rhine, I felt strong for the trip, so I beat it for Cologne in my Vauxhall limousine and missed my opportunity of giving a frank expression of my views. I have a feeling that had I been present at that Church Reform session I would have gotten sufficient off my chest to have at least caused the Archbishop to remember our little session. Perhaps he will kindly accept a copy of this book instead as a more mature expression on the reforms needed in church.

In language more forceful than polite I had told my parson's mess mates that the Church of England, speaking generally, was as dead as the busted city of Ypres and that she would continue

THE DESTINY OF AMERICA

so until her archbishops, bishops and clergy realized what Jesus meant when he said (Matt. 21:43), "The kingdom of God shall be taken from you [Jews], and given to a nation bringing forth the fruits thereof"; until they realized that there was nothing on this habitable globe as certain as the "more sure word of prophecy"; and until they carried out the injunction to "search the Scriptures" and "find the sheep that were lost," "the sheep of my pasture," (and this flock are men, the Lost Ten Tribes of Israel); until then, I told them, their church would remain as dead as a doornail to the essential needs of the people for Bible enlightenment.

When, however, they see this great truth, as they are due to see very shortly, then indeed will the Bible become the living Word of God; their churches will be filled with thronging multitudes hungering and thirsting for the Truth; and they will be in a position to expound to intelligent listeners in a practical way that would in no sense detract from the glory of God, as revealed by Him both through the actions of men and nations upon earth now, and as disclosed through both the Old and New Testaments. Then indeed, shall we see that outpouring of the Holy Spirit predicted by Peter, in Acts 2:17, and the casting aside of the vail which caused blindness in part to happen to Israel until the fullness of the Gentiles came in,—which arrived in 1917 when Britain won the Holy Land from heathen Turkey or Edom. God said His people Israel would redeem Jerusalem. Britain redeemed it, therefore Britain is Israel, as God is never mistaken, seeing the end from the beginning. How the church to-day ducks this historical fact is beyond my comprehension.

Wake up Christian Churches!

Well, what about a waymark for the younger brother, Ephraim (England)? Has he a totem pole showing where he came from? He surely has. In 1819 Mehemet Ali of Egypt presented Cleopatra's Needle to the British Government. Why, I wonder? Why didn't he give it to Italy, Germany, France, Russia or Spain? Apparently when given it was a white elephant, not the kind with a capacity for eating hay all night and all day that de Wolf Hopper used to sing about, but still "some elephant." I can imagine the consternation among British officialdom on how to get the "blooming thing 'ome," because the wooden ships in those days were not built to carry elongated pebbles of its size on the open sea. Apparently it laid on the Egyptian sands for fifty-eight years, after it was gifted unto the English, as the records show that in 1877 it was loaded into a special clyindrical ship built for it, and started for England, but was lost and supposed to have foundered in the Bay of Biscay. I had heard of Rev. Dr. Wild stating from his pulpit that it would not be lost forever, but would yet be found

THE DESTINY OF AMERICA 63

and taken to England as a witness of God's care and oversight of His chosen seed, Israel, located in the Brith-ish or Covenant Isles.

Evidently the Creator and Governor of this world had a different plan for this waymark than dropping it to the bottom of the sea in Biscay Bay, for, after floating around for some weeks, wrecked and lost, it was sighted, taken in tow, and finally landed at its destination, and to-day stands in the heart of the greatest city of the world, on the Thames Embankment, London, not only as a mark of the place of origin of Ephraim, Israel, but also of the brotherhood between the United States of America and Great Britain, offspring peoples of Joseph's two sons, born in Egypt before the Exodus. Whom God hath joined together, let no man put asunder—neither Sinn Feiner or pro-German. As children, the two lads playing around these monuments likely claimed one each, and to-day they have them in reality, one in New York and the other in London.

For fear that you may kick at having only *one* waymark for so great a people, may I be permitted to point out that America and Britain have *all* Israel's heraldry between them; your coins and seals of state carry the marks of your origin. In 1879 Rev. Joseph Wild, preaching in Brooklyn Church, N. Y., gave the marks of Manasseh possessed by America, and more recently Rev. J. H. Allen, of California, has published a very readable small book called *The National Number and Heraldry of the United States of America,* price forty cents. I mention the price because, if you are not Scotch, perhaps you will venture this small amount for it. I can guarantee it will be as stimulating to that wee streak of vanity we all possess as any highball ever swallowed.

What a strange thing the mind is! The second I wrote that word "highball" my thought switched to a scene in that quaint and beautiful old town of Bailleul in Northern France, now unfortunately level with the ground, where an army corps had its headquarters in the winter of 1915. The army was not then as dry as it became in 1918, and every visitor to an engineer's mess was invited to "wet his whistle." One always-welcomed-Major, now a Brigadier-General, took his initial dose for "wet feet," and when the bottle was pushed his way a second time, with the invitation "have another," he would remark, "well, a pigeon can't fly with one wing. Here's to you!" I may say that the aforementioned chap usually had a supply of wings that made him feel like a real bird ere he flew for another turn at duty among the shells.

You will remember that your nation set up in business of their own in 1776. Due perhaps to your faulty school books, you may not remember or know that the bulk of British people in England were as opposed to taxation for America as were

THE DESTINY OF AMERICA

the British people then in America who rebelled, and so strong was this feeling in England that the English king,—one removed from being made in Germany!—had to pay Hessians to come over to fight against you; as British soldiers would neither volunteer nor enlist.

Your American author, Owen Wister, has written a splendid book called *A Straight Deal or the Ancient Grudge,* which every American and Britisher should read. He points out how America, as well as England, has land-grabbed from the lesser breeds without the law, first from the Indians time after time (though America had to break treaty after treaty to do so), then Florida, Texas, California, Arizona, Nevada, Alaska, Cuba, Phillipines, etc. What Owen Wister does not point out, or perhaps does not know, is that you are only fulfilling your God-given destiny and taking on your inheritance in settling the coasts and waste places of the earth; your treaties were overruled time after time to make you colonize what was then a waste, the southern half of North America.

"Ask of me, and I shall give thee [Israel] the heathen for thine inheritance, and the uttermost parts of the earth for thy possession." (Ps. 2:8.)

"Thus saith the Lord, In an acceptable time have I heard thee [Israel], and in a day of salvation have I helped thee: and I will preserve thee, and give thee for a covenant of the people, to establish the earth, to cause to inherit the desolate heritages." (Isa. 49:8.)

It was a large contract but our forefathers have worked at it for hundreds of years; your Puritan Forefathers knew what it meant to establish their section of the "desolate heritages," and furthermore, they believed that they were fulfilling the above particular prophecy and they believed that they were what I say you are, God's Israel, as I will try to show you later on. Their settlement was a little one, but, as was prophesied in Isaiah 60:22, "A little one shall become a thousand, and a small one a strong nation." You started, a little one, and you have become a strong nation.

Well, I started in on waymarks, and I've drifted away from them on these numerous sidelines that to me are so interesting that I set them down, hoping they may help formulate your opinion as to who you are, where you come from and what your job is.

When America won its predicted Independence, what do you suppose they put on their Great Seal, which was adopted by Congress, June 20, 1782? Of course you don't know. Manasseh means in Hebrew *"forgetfulness"* and Americans have forgotten the place of their origin where Joseph's son was born in the city of Memphis, a few miles from the greatest wonder of the world, the Great Pyramid of Gizeh with its capstone missing. The Creator is not a forgetter, however, and the reverse side of your Great Seal

THE DESTINY OF AMERICA 67

has as its main feature an unfinished Pyramid with the All-seeing Eye above it, as another sign or waymark of their home land by which Americans may locate their identity.

America and Britain, between them, have all the Hebrew Israelitish heraldry fairly evenly distributed, so its up to you to polish up your forgetter and know who you are, how you got here, and what God's plan is for your next, greatest and last war.

Some of us at the Front thought you took "a long time" to get into the recent disturbance in France and Flanders, and we are a bit anxious that you do not let it become a habit. Despite all the talk of "peace, peace, where there is no peace," some twenty-eight wars are going on as I write this. Despite the man-made League of Nations, made apparently without God's guidance or will, made contrary to the divine plan for handling world-wide problems and bringing peace and goodwill on earth, it will not stop the Bible war schedule being carried out and on time. War is not over; the League of Nations will not stop war. Armageddon has yet to be fought and America must not again be a tailender. If they get wise to who they are and what the Creator's plan is for their next war, they would never lay down the keel of another dreadnought at forty million dollars per ship, because these ships will be wasted and the millions spent on each of them might as well be thrown in mid ocean. More dreadnoughts for America's next war will be quite as useful for her needs as a cow is for climbing telegraph poles, and no more. General Leonard Wood in the January, 1921, *Metropolitan* describes your blind pre-war condition so accurately that I quote it for your future consideration and guidance:

> "We had the men, we had the money too! But although God had given us eyes to see, ears to hear, memory to carry and an intelligence to apply the lesson of all time, apparently our eyes had not seen, our ears had not heard, our memory not carried, nor had our intelligence applied the lessons of the past! It was slow in applying those of the present. There was no thought-out plan of action."

General Wood knew whereof he spake as well as any man on this American Continent. Yet what is your thought-out plan of action to-day? You don't even know that Armageddon has yet to be fought! Whoever christened you Manasseh certainly must have had foreknowledge of your long suit, "Forgetfulness."

It has been said by some of your American papers that you were caught with your hands tied in the last war, though your politicians had many years notice from some of your naval officers of how things were heading. In future, do not tempt Providence overmuch, because France and Brother John may not be in a position to hold on and save the world again while Brother Jonathan's politicians are deciding whether or not he is too "proud to fight," and are hushing up everything, trying to be neutral in thought, word and deed, with Europe being murdered by a ruthless soul-destroying antichristian combination out to hamstring that world liberty and freedom which America has always stood for.

Many, many years ago Germany invented the poison gas of higher criticism and year after year her ministers kicked away first this, that and the other prop of peoples' belief in the inspiration of the Bible until Martin Luther would not recognize as Christian their creed that might is right, when made in Germany. When made in France, England or at Versailles, of course, might is not right. Their poison gas during the war was no more deadly to the Allies than their poison gas of higher criticism was on their own people before the war and not one half as deadly as their world-wide propaganda against Britain in Russia, China, India, Egypt, Ireland, United States and elsewhere. Germany well understands that if she can separate Brother John and Brother Jonathan, she may still have a chance to dominate the world, and the world has never seen such efforts to drive us apart as are now on foot through their spy system again working overtime all over America and Canada; "but the wise shall understand."

When your fighting men got to the Front, they showed that they were the equal of Canadians, Australians, New Zealanders, South Africans and that staunch old backbone of all the armies, "Tommy," Tommy from England, Ireland, Scotland and from the uttermost parts of the earth.

Britain's call to her children and their response was, to my mind, the most sublime picture ever presented on this sphere: men in millions, giving up wealth, position, ease, comfort, their wives and children and everything that men have held worth while in this life, to fight for God in France and Belgium, in order that freedom should not perish from the face of this earth. I used to pass these fighting men marching up to the Front in the winter of 1916 drenched with the downpouring rain and sleet, foot slogging through the mud on their way up to the trenches, that were then knee-deep in mud, slush, dirt and filth. Only those who have been through that sordid ordeal, the winter of 1915-1916, can ever know the misery to our fighting troops of that winter in front of Ypres. One would never consider for a minute putting a dog or a pig or any animal into the quarters our men held through those trying days and months and years. I felt like taking my hat off to them every time I saw them marching in, well knowing that from ten to fifty per cent. of them would not come out, except possibly on a stretcher. I felt that some Power greater than our ordinary clay caused these millions of men to serve God, King and Country in those heartrending years. Again, I am off the main track and on a siding.

Manasseh (Hebrew for forgetfulness) was the thirteenth tribe of Israel, as Ephraim, given the birthright, took his father's (Joseph's) place as the twelfth tribe. Has America any waymarks indicating that they are the thirteenth tribe of Israel?

1. The Pyramid on your government's Great Seal has just *thirteen* tiers of stone.
2. There are *thirteen* bars or palways on the shield which your eagle holds as there were thirteen strips of land in Palestine.
3. There are thirteen arrows in the eagle's right claw.
4. There are *thirteen* leaves in the olive branch in the left claw thus symbolizing that you are a branch of that good olive tree. (Romans 11:24.)
5. *Thirteen* stars above the eagle's head.
6. *E. Pluribus Unum* has thirteen letters and means one out of many (one tribe out of many tribes of Israel and the thirteenth tribe.)

If you read J. H. Allen's book* you will locate just thirteen different thirteens that mark Manasseh as the thirteenth tribe. You did not

---

**The National Number and Heraldry of the United States of America.*

set up in national business until you had thirteen Brith-ish or Covenant colonies to start up with (why not twelve or fourteen?) and you never changed your heraldic number thirteen when you added to your states except by adding additional stars to your flag.

Jacob had twelve children.

1. Reuben
2. Simeon
3. Levi
4. Judah
5. Asher
6. Naphtali
7. Zebulon
8. Gad
9. Dan
10. Issachar
11. Benjamin
12. Joseph—12 Ephraim
             13 Manasseh

As Joseph had two sons, a double portion was given him for Ephraim and Manasseh, thus making the thirteen. Now Jacob set Ephraim before Manasseh, this making him twelfth and making Manasseh the thirteenth son and tribe. If you do not like your number, please don't blame me, as I did not originate it. I just mention it because it is certainly a lucky number for the United States of America and further it is your heraldic number. See Genesis 48:5 for a description of how they were put on the same basis as Reuben and Simeon and the other sons of Jacob that became tribes of Israel.

"And now thy two sons, Ephraim and Manasseh, which were born unto thee in the land of Egypt before I came unto thee in Egypt, are mine; as Reuben and Simeon, they shall be mine."

CHAPTER IV.

1. When Moses marched out of Egypt, they standardized the British "hollow square."
2. The banner Americans and English marched under.
3. How Johnnie Bull got the name Engleland.
4. The French can never understand the Englishman, but can the Yankee, Canadian or Australian.
5. How the Englishmen look to many outsiders.
6. John Bull got his Drinkatite in early Bible days. Does he still retain it?
7. Has Ephraim (England) changed his spots? Not that you would notice!
8. Are British regular soldier officers a stubborn stiffnecked generation? Try them.
9. A typical wounded Tommy and his high standard of duty.
10. Tommy from the uttermost parts of the earth, with God's help, won the war.
11. John Bull a lovable brother when you understand the character behind his mask.
12. What British civil servants and soldiers and sailors have done for the heathen for centuries!
13. President Harding's views of the profound duties God has thrust upon us Anglo-Saxon-Celts.

CHAPTER IV.

Moses led the children of Israel out of Egypt about 1492 B.C., and the same number of years after Christ, the American Continent was discovered by a Spanish Jew, and it has proved no less a land of deliverance to millions of Israelites, Jews and Gentiles alike.

When leaving Egypt, the people marched in sections or groups of three tribes on each side of the Ark of the Tabernacle, and here we get the first example of the British "hollow square," used by their fighting troops for centuries to repel attacks.

Ephraim, Manasseh, and Benjamin, children and grandchildren of Jacob through Rachel, marched on the west side of the Tabernacle under a banner having a bull's head on it. The word "bull" in Hebrew is *Engle,* and the tribe of Ephraim later, in their wanderings up and down and across Europe, gradually came to be called by the name of their flag, "Engles" or "Angles." When Ephraim and their followers invaded Britain, does it seem strange that they called the section of the Covenant land they took possession of Engle or Bull Land, and that the name has stuck down through the ages in the names of Johnnie Bull and his country Engle (or Bull) Land? Also when they came to America they established a new Engle land in Massachusetts. As the Assyrians, the modern Huns, have run true to type through several thousand years, so surely does Johnnie Bull or Ephraim carry down from early Bible days his then prevailing characteristics.

To-day the average Frenchman and most Europeans think the typical Englishman is a proud, haughty mortal, impressed with his own national superiority, which he shows in a manner and with an air that offends them all; but the aforementioned Englishman neither comprehends nor bothers about it. On the other hand, the Yankee, Canadian or Australian, has quite as large an opinion of his particular importance to this world and will tell you all about it without any side or effort to suppress himself, in a way that isn't done "at 'ome" and that shocks the Englishman to the core; but which the Frenchman and European understands and is not offended at. Why?

Isaiah 28:1 says, "Woe to the crown of pride, to the drunkards of Ephraim," and in the 3rd verse for fear they should be overlooked, these characteristics are again repeated: "The crown of pride, the drunkards of Ephraim, shall be trodden under feet"—as they were at the time that chapter refers to. O, drinking stiff-necked

Ephraim of Bible days, how are you now? Well, after over three years close association with him in all his moods and tenses, I'm of the opinion that he hasn't changed much more than the leopard has his spots. His crown of pride he still wears with an effort hardly concealed, to make himself believe he has none. He would have his drink until he became drunken three thousand years ago and he will have it yet. Some pubs in London are to-day filled with drinking and drunken women. The bulk of the hardy upstanding yeomanry of centuries ago are gone and the war showed such a large percentage of recruits of "class 3" calibre that it appalled the country. Had it not been for the old-fashioned lion hearts discovered in those "class 3" physiques, and brought to the surface by the war, it would have fared much worse with our Allies.

I once asked a war correspondent why it was the newspapers always plastered Canadians, Australians, New Zealanders, and occasionally the Scotch and Irish with peans of praise for their good fighting work and hardly mentioned the English who formed over sixty-two per cent. of all the British armies on all our fronts. Well, he rather thought, you know, that they didn't expect it. They sure didn't get it anyway! Many times I've felt cheap at seeing only Canadian troops mentioned by the newspapers in a fight when I knew that three-quarters of the fighting, and splendid fighting, was done by English troops on our right and left. What the English men, and women too, from Devonshire and the ports of England did on our merchantmen and hospital ships and navy, to keep open the sea lanes of traffic and supplies for all the armies and for transporting American troops, was superb in its daring. Some of these men and women had ship after ship sink under them, sunk by the German sea pirates in their submarines. But when saved, they went again to the nearest port and signed up and so carried on their share in helping Britain win the war. These English civilians shouldered a most hazardous work, that made unrecognized *heroes* of them all without either glory or praise.

Drink and its attendant and following evils, bad living conditions, poor housing, etc., has been a national sin and evil in Ephraim (England) for ages, and is and has been and will continue to be paid for at the highest market price—as is always the way. You cannot break God's laws on booze, and get away with it any more than you could with slavery. The mills of God grind slowly but they grind, and the old order has not been changed since it was said, "Whatsoever a man soweth, that shall he also reap." What crop can Ephraim expect from their liquor bills of 1919 and 1920? Mr. Geo. R. Wilson of the United Kingdom Alliance published, in the *Daily Mail Year Book,* statistics showing an in-

THE DESTINY OF AMERICA

crease of 60 per cent. absolute alcohol used in 1919 over that used in 1918.

In 1918 the permitted output of beer, per annum, was 12,500,000 standard barrels at the time of the Armistice; by June of 1919 it had risen to 25,454,000 barrels; and since then it has been unrestricted and has increased accordingly. Beer and wine have increased 70 per cent. and spirits 43 per cent. In 1918 in the United Kingdom they spent £259,300,000 against £166,000,000 in 1913 and £386,600,000 for 1919. At $4.80 per pound this would be $1,854,680,000 for beer, wine, and spirits for one year.* It hardly seems enough? Only £13.14 shillings per head of population over twenty-one years of age including a large population of abstainers,—a tax equal to $65.00 a head for booze per annum. Who but England could or would stand for it? Do you think Ephraim has changed his spots much since Isaiah's time when he was labelled "drunken"? "Ephraim is joined to idols: let him alone." Hosea 4:17 is apparently true to-day. Yes, you can take it that tribal characteristics do pass from generation to generation, in Israel as elsewhere, and that Johnnie Bull has not been weaned from lapping up more fire-water, strong beer, porter and ale than is good for the space beneath his waistcoat. America has gone dry, as has

---

*Statistics from *Boston News Bureau*.

Canada legally, though still semiwet actually. Brother John will have to join up or be left behind through the inefficiency generated by alcohol. Well might England follow the advice His Majesty gave them some years ago to "wake up."

If you wish to know if "stiff-necked" and "stubborn generation" still applies, just live with his regular soldiers for a few years and try to inoculate them with a few new ideas on how to get on with the war. They are as impervious to new ideas as the Sphinx is to pin pricks. I don't know if all the stiff-necked stubborn ones foregathered as regular soldiers or whether it is the army that breeds that particular brand of stubbornness, but they surely were plentiful thereabouts, in my locality at any rate. 'Tis probably this same stubbornness rightly directed that has enabled British soldiers and armies to break the back of every menace to which the world has been subject for hundreds of years.

When, however, it comes to giving you a square deal, commend me to the aforementioned stiffnecked chap, who, if it wasn't done in Cromwell's time, sees many reasons why it should not be done now. He does not praise you for the finest bit of work you ever did, but then, he doesn't look for praise himself, and he doesn't get any of it either from his superiors! It is bad form, you know, to give vent to your real feelings; your face must be as calm and unexpressive as a "ball of yarn." Bless me, but I used to shock some of those red-tabbed chaps with major-general written all over them, when giving vent to my feelings and opinions in good old American "langwidge" picked up in Wisconsin in the early nineties, handling Swedes and Finlanders; and not entirely disposed of since, as it frequently crops out on provocation at unexpected times, I regret to state.

That same stubborn persistence is what makes our British Tommy and his officers such splendid fighters. They haven't an idea that they can be licked; they are out to win and they just hang on until the last shot is fired, and then some, and its a sorry day when Tommy is not cheerful over the toughest kind of hard luck.

Here is a fair sample. One day in the fall of 1916 I was looking at a road on the Hospital Grounds near Contay, in the Somme Area. The officer commanding was receiving several hundred wounded from the Courcelette fight. I met a walk-case hobbling along the duckboard walk—a sorry sight to look at.

"Well, Tommy, it looks like Blighty for yours," I said,—Blighty was heaven in those days.

I wonder if I can picture him for you. He looked forty, dressed in khaki caked with clay and chalk mud from his boots to his neck. He had no hat, his head was all bandaged up, also his neck and his chin; one side of his face bulging out of the bandage was three inches bigger than the other and the cheek and eye were black and blue as if he had been kicked by a mule; his left arm was not in his tunic, but in a sling; he limped badly, and his pants were slit open from below the knee to the thigh, with white bandage and blood showing through the split trousers. He had a big tag tied to his tunic giving his name, number, regiment, what dope he had had, if any, and where he was billed for; so that if he dropped anywhere, they had his particulars, while he could give them, and on he would go. He looked so battered up that I asked,

"Well, Tommy, what did you get?"

Speaking through his closed teeth he said, "Well, sir, the worst is this 'ere shot through my cheek, that took out all my lower teeth on the right side and came out through the side of my neck."

Then there were two scalp wounds with shrapnel, chin cut, wrist broken or sprained—I've forgotten which—and a bullet had gone clean through the muscles of his right leg above the knee. There he was limping along the duckboards, waiting for the ambulance to take him to the hospital train, and no one paying any more attention to him, after he was through the receiving tent, than if he was an army mule. I'm afraid I must have forgotten my temporary army training and let a little feeling slip into my voice when I remarked,

"Well, you sure got a full dose."

"Oh! I'm damn lucky, sir! All my mates were killed."

Can you beat it for real spirit? Tommy, Tommy, from the uttermost parts of the earth, with his unquenchable spirit won the war, with God's help, then only after every Anglo-Saxon nation had offered national prayers asking God's help and guidance in those stern days in the spring and summer of 1918 on the Amiens Front. Get that? You must, because it is the key to the offensive that won the war!

Most people at home would feel that they were badly used under foregoing conditions; but there was Tommy, asking no favors and surely getting none, and feeling that he was "damn lucky" to be alive. All his mates were dead, torn to pieces by shells, drowned in mud and water-filled shell-holes as they tried to navigate their way back to the dressing stations. He could look after himself, wounded as he was; and his duty was to do so to his full limit and until he dropped—then it became the duty of the stretcher-bearers, and they took on the job if they saw him fall, or if they found him.

That's another thing for which we have to take off our hats to Johnnie Bull. He is strong on duty—duty that must be done; and he is strong for law, order and liberty. I grew to love him like a brother, because I could see him as he never could see himself. Bless his whole tribe, with his faults and his strong fair-dealing proclivities! He has carried his section of God's people forward by a way he knew not, and will yet lead them still further forward until the millennium ushers in a newer order, which I hope many of us will live to see (after we finish Armageddon); because, though I am no "spring chicken," I have hopes of serving in Armageddon as a roadbuilder and I hope to start a few years ahead instead of having to do everything in the heat of war, as it could be done so much easier now, just as Fritz built his strategical railways to Belgian and French borders before 1914.

The British regular army has on their list doing active service in forsaken outposts of the Empire, such as the hills of India, etc., men of independent means by the thousand, who leave wife and family and serve solely at the call of duty. They accept as a regular diet what we civilians turned our hands to for a few years at the call of our King or, in your case, at the call of your country. What the British regular officer and British civil servants have done for the heathen for centuries is beyond praise; and mark this: you, Manasseh, are quite as much benefited by it as is John Bull & Company, because wherever Britain paves the way at the cost of her

THE DESTINY OF AMERICA

treasure and lives, America is as free to follow and trade, as is Britain, Canada or other sections of our glorious heritage. May blessings rest on those thousands of civil servants and officers of His Majesty's army and navy, who for several hundred years have been and are now carrying along the Creator's work in those waste places of the earth and among the heathen, carrying with them justice and fairdealing, honor, truth and duty and goodwill to all men, be they black, white or yellow!

President-elect Warren G. Harding wrote to the Chairman of the Sulgrave Institute recently a letter that places him in the statesman class.

"Destiny has made it a historical fact that the English-speaking peoples have been the instrument through which civilization has been flung to the far corners of the globe.

"I am impressed not so much by the glory that English-speakng peoples may take to themselves, as by the profound duties that God has thrust upon them—duties of being restrained, tolerant and just.

"These duties will find their greatest recognition in a united, unshakable friendship and understanding and oneness of purpose—not for the exclusion from brotherhood of others, but for a better brotherhood flowing towards others."

Israel was to be God's servant, His instrument to take civilization, law, and ordered liberty to the ends of the earth. If, as President Harding says, "English-speaking peoples have been the instrument" to do just what Israel was to do, then, the English-speaking people are Israel. President Warren G. Harding, elected head of God's "great people," has spoken the truth.

Your President plainly recognizes that God has thrust this duty upon us English-speaking peoples; and he does well. I wonder if he will be able to recognize the connection between his words and these inspired words of the Bible:

> "But thou, Israel, art my servant, Jacob whom I have chosen, the seed of Abraham my friend. Thou whom I have taken from the ends of the earth, and called thee from the chief men thereof, and said unto thee, Thou art my servant; I have chosen thee, and not cast thee away. Fear thou not; for I am with thee: be not dismayed; for I am thy God: I will strengthen thee; yea, I will help thee; yea, I will uphold thee with the right hand of my righteousness. . . . For I, the Lord thy God, will hold thy right hand, saying unto thee, Fear not; I will help thee. Fear not, thou worm Jacob, and ye men of Israel; I will help thee, saith the Lord, and thy redeemer, the Holy One of Israel . . . and thou shalt rejoice in the Lord, and shalt glory in the Holy One of Israel." (Isa. 41: 8-10, 13, 14, 16.)

When President Harding realizes who we are then that better brotherhood, that light to all peoples which we were commissioned to carry will get the impulse that has been lacking up to date in America's dealings with the world outside her borders.

The blindness in part which was to happen to national Israel until the fullness of the Gentiles came in is now lifted and President-elect Harding and every other American is in a position to say as Paul did, "I also am an Israelite, of the seed of Abraham," who was God's friend.

CHAPTER V.

1. Ambassador Brand Whitlock served America and the world.
2. Nurse Edith Cavell's last words.
3. The Prussian (Assyrian) never can understand Anglo-Saxons.
4. A hospital sample of their poison gas "Kultur."
5. More leisure for clear thinking at the Front.
6. Like Topsy, has the world just happened?
7. How we grew to hate beautiful moonlight nights at the Front.
8. The souls of the stoutest men in America will quake in the years coming.
9. Has the Creator a business plan for America and the world?
10. Are we running on schedule time to His plan?
11. Why I keep my hair short and join the Navy League.
12. Israel mentioned in prophetic despatches 2,543 times.
13. The Bible indictment of the shepherds or ministers of God's flock.
14. Man is naturally a religious animal.
15. Every date in the Bible checks with astronomical time.

THE DESTINY OF AMERICA

16. The law Moses gave the American section of Israel.
17. America and Britain fulfilling Moses' prophecies literally.
18. Our enemies open and secret have been found liars as was promised by the inspired prophets of old.
19. Manasseh, "Forgetfulness" is America's tribal name. Are they living up to it?

CHAPTER V.

One of the most pathetic statements ever made fell from the lips of Nurse Edith Cavell under sentence of death in a German prison. She was so thankful for those ten weeks she was in jail, for the quiet, and the time to think and rest. Life had been so hurried. She expressed truly what most mortals feel as we gallop with rush and bustle through this hurried life of striving and strife. And all for what?

The following report was made by the British chaplain, H. Sterling Gohan, to Mr. Brand Whitlock, the United States Ambassador who served America and the whole civilized world so well, during the war years at Brussels. A charming man with the most winsome of manners, he secured many favors from Germany, due to his personality. I had met him first when he was giving Toledo, Ohio, good government as its mayor and again after the Armistice when I was welcomed in his sanctum at Brussels; and I succeeded for an hour in chasing some of the brain fag from a very, very tired war-worn American public servant, who held on to his job amidst discouragements that would have daunted most people.

Report of Edith Cavell's Execution by Germany
Made to United States Ambassador

"On Monday evening, the 11th of October, I was admitted by special passport from the German authorities, to the prison of St. Giles where Miss Edith Cavell had been confined for ten weeks. The final sentence of Death had been given that afternoon.

"To my astonishment and relief, I found my friend perfectly calm and resigned, but this could not lessen the tenderness and intensity of feeling on either part during the last interview of almost an hour.

"Her first words to me were upon a matter concerning herself personally, but the solemn asseveration which accompanied them was made expressly in the light of God and Eternity. She then added that she wished all her friends to know that she willingly gave her life for her country, and said, 'I have no fear nor shrinking: I have seen Death so often that it is not strange or fearful to me.' She further said *'I thank God for this ten weeks quiet before the end. Life has always been so hurried* and full of difficulty. This time of rest has been a great mercy. They have all been kind to me here, but I would say, standing in the view of God and Eternity, I realize that Patriotism is not enough. . . . I must have no hatred towards any one.'

"We partook of the Holy Communion together and she received the Gospel message of consolation with all her heart. At the close of the little service I began to repeat the words 'Abide with me' and she joined softly in the end. We sat quietly talking until it was time for her to go. She gave me parting messages for relatives and friends. She spoke of her soul's need at the moment and she received the assurance of God's words as only a Christian can do. Then I said 'Good-bye,' and she smiled and said, 'We shall meet again!'

"The German Military Chaplain was with her at the end and afterwards gave her Christian burial. He told me:

'She was brave and bright to the last. She professed her Christian Faith and that she was glad to die for her country. She died like a hero.'

H. STERLING GOHAN,
British Chaplain, Brussels.

Thus died a quiet, thoughtful, unemotional English heroine, a martyr to duty, a martyr to Germany's system of frightfulness. Could Assyrian Germany ever understand our Anglo-Saxon breed, they never would have shot a nurse, a woman who had nursed their own soldiers as well as Belgians, French and British. Her death caused more men to enlist against such brutality all over Christendom, than any single appeal made to the hearts of white men.

There are thousands who look back upon the years spent in those semi-jails in France and Belgium, dugouts, saps, trenches, and billets, with the A.E.F., B.E.F., and C.E.F., who, like Nurse Cavell, were most thankful for the chance it gave them to rest and get their thoughts up to date.

With Death looking for you or your friends from any and all points of the compass, from above and below, from in front and behind, we still had thousands of opportunities, more than ever came to us in our business at home, to calmly think and wonder over the riddle of this universe. What was the meaning of this stupendous war with its millions of lives passing forward to their next stopping station; with the awful waste of cities; of forests; of fertile lands; of munitions; and the waste of those splendid fighting men who, at the call of the wee small voice within, took upon themselves fighting tasks under conditions such as men never before in the history of the world have fought and held and won?

I remember one morning going into a Canadian casualty clearing station at Remy Siding, just behind Poperinghe, to see why a Padre had pinched several of my road menders. He took me around behind the semi-permanent hospital huts, and I saw a dozen huge tents with their sides all rolled up, so that every possible breath of air could reach within. There lay eight hundred gas-poisoned soldiers, who had come in during the night; the regular hospital cots being full, the large tents had to be hastily improvised to accommodate them.

The battalion had been up doing front-line work at night. They had left their rifles, greatcoats, and gas-masks a short distance in the rear when the Huns sent over one of those choice marks of his Kultur, poison gas, and it drenched the whole battalion with its deadly fumes. As I looked upon those hundreds of stricken men on cots and stretchers and on the tent floors, so many with distorted faces, frothing from the mouth, their bodies writhing, their faces turning green and black, gasping for their last few breaths of life, those men, who a few hours before had been pictures of health, now dying before our eyes like flies, one wondered anew what was God's plan in this war? When would it end and how? Sherman knew that war was hell; but this war developed more kinds of hell than Sherman or civilized people could possibly have conceived of until they learned to what lengths German Kultur could go in infamy while endeavouring to shove their mailed fist down our throats and so prove that might is right.

The Padre had taken my road-menders to dig the last resting-place—a long open trench six feet wide—for fifty-two men who had died that morning, as he only had men sufficient to dig graves for their average death rate of from five to ten per day.

Since 1884 I had believed that that inspired Book, our much neglected Bible, contained the history of God's chosen people, Israel; that they were the "stone kingdom" of Daniel's vision; and that they were God's battle-axe and shield and His weapons of war to subdue the Babylon nations of earth opposed to His rule. Do you wonder that during the war I became interested anew in trying to study the divine plan for the universe, the mystery of God?

It seems strange, but it is true, that life at the Front at times left every business man

THE DESTINY OF AMERICA

there *more leisure to think,* with a clear mind, than he ever before possessed; one was not bothered about payrolls, profits, rising freight rates, the "Red" menace, the strikers' union, irate shareholders, or the thousand and one daily and hourly disturbing things that drift into one's office at home in a big city. He just did his job, whatever it was; thanked Providence if he had a dry billet, behind a brick wall if possible, to protect him from flying shrapnel and air bombs; hoped that the moonlight schedule would be cloudy, because Fritz always sent his bombing planes over every bright night; kept his prayers said fairly well up to date, if he said any; and left the rest to his Maker with a peace in his soul that passed the understanding of our friends at home.

Every moonlight night at the Front, during 1917 and 1918, Fritz made a point of air-raiding trips over our back as well as front areas, until we grew to hate the moon as the devil is alleged to hate holy water. On occasions they made as many as six raids throughout the night and it took strong nerves and a tired body to sleep through them and get a night's rest for next day's work.

Often when walking home to my billet on those beautiful moonlight nights, as I looked up to the heavens and saw those ten thousand stars, each star a world, I wondered how it was possible for any man who could run a business or a section of one to think that those wonderful worlds ran on schedule without a plan and without a creator. Such a man certainly had more faith than I possessed to think that such a thing were possible or that this one world of God's big universe "just grew" like Topsy and ran itself without a Creator or without His laws and guidance. How long would your little business run without an executive head or without rules and plans for carrying on laid down by its head? Then what about the universe?

I thought then and many times since that if our business men could only get that peace of mind, that repose of soul that we enjoyed at the Front, they would be able to see things in their proper perspective; and that if they had God's plan for our national guidance in their think boxes, they would not need to worry much over the "Reds" or the dozens of other ills that will afflict the whole world during the next fifteen years—years that will try the souls of the stoutest men of this American Continent, because it is plainly foretold that the world is to go through such a time of trouble as never was on earth before, of which the late war was but a preliminary.

At present every business man knows this old world is almost upside down and turned inside out, and millions wonder what will happen next and how order can ever be restored from the

THE DESTINY OF AMERICA

present (1920) chaotic condition all over the world. On this continent, less than on any other, it is true at present, but even here there is seething unrest ready to explode in spots.

We are in the habit of looking upon many of our big captains of industry with considerable awe, men who succeed in planning and working huge plants for production outputs at the lowest unit costs, etc. We think they are "some men" and we, so to speak, take off our hats to our Schwabs, Fords, Hoovers, Morgans, and the rest of them (I understand there are some who do not take off their hats to the men who scrambled your railroads for several years,—but let that go.)

Well, I'll bet not one in a thousand knows that there is a plan, a business plan, foretold and laid down thousands of years ago and that we are working to that divine plan and schedule in our wars, our smashing of nations, our pulling down of kings and dynasties and strange as it may seem, we are working on time even to the year and to the month and the day according to these prophecies foretold thousands of years ago. Sounds a bit fishy doesn't it? But, as we observed before, truth is stranger than fiction, and this is truth.

About eight years ago, returing from a Mediterranean trip, sitting next to a chunky little Johnnie Bull Englishman on board ship we had many talks about gardening, yachting, etc. One evening after three days at sea, I told him about the English being the Ephraim tribe of Israel and was a bit surprised to note that he was not properly shocked. We discussed it pro and con and finally turning to me, he said, "You know, my old parson (who is a long-haired chap) has been giving me that dope for the last fifteen years, but I never before heard of a short-haired intelligent business man who had any faith or took any stock in it!"

We adjourned to the smoking room and over a hot toddy, or was it two?—he made me a life member or vice-admiral or something or other in the British Navy League at 20 quid a throw. Being Scotch I remember that part of it as I had to mail him a cheque when I got home. I also remember that I tried to head him off promising, that if he would join Mrs. Pankhurst's Suffrage League, which at that time was fairly busy heaving half bricks at Members of Parliament and otherwise making their lives a bit uncertain, that I would join his Navy League in any capacity for which my age, big feet and fondness for water would qualify me. Not carried!

Having tried this Anglo-Saxon-Israel Identity on numerous friends and acquaintances, I have noted with real enjoyment the quick searching glance they all give you to see if you have been drinking,—and in these arid days! Then you see that far-away look steal into their eyes, denoting that you have them off their feet and in deep water and they are afraid you'll ask them some question that will show that the Bible and they are strangers. Not that I blame them, because, without the proper key, the Bible is about as interesting to a business man as an Algebra is to a ten-year-old school boy.

Israel is the Hebrew for "ruling with God" and is mentioned in despatches in the Bible some 2543 times, and over two-thirds of the Old and New Testament are written about Israel. Without the key and history showing who and where the nation Israel is, a fine healthy chance any ordinary man has to understand where the prophets are heading him; and yet that is where our churches and parsons leave us. The church is not mentioned that I have seen in the Old Testament and only 110 times in the New; so the parsons who would appropriate to the church the promises made to the nation Israel by the Creator would, except for this ignorance, seem to me to qualify under Revelation 22:18, 19. Most ministers I've talked it over with know as much about Israel as a cat knows about his grandfather! They can give you several conjectures as to Israel being Jews, but unfortunately they are surmises only. They have guessed wrong, with the result that the living Word of God is as dead as a doornail to the average business man, the man who is accustomed to attend church regularly; but the blind leaders of the blind have him where he thinks he cannot use his everyday methods of applying his gray matter to the subject and reason his way out or see his way out, and the fewness of these business men in the churches all over the land is the proof of this wrong reading and teaching of God's Word to His People, Israel, by these blind shepherds. If my parson friends think this language too strong may I plead in extenuation that I'm only reiterating a small part of what the Bible calls them. I venture to think that they would pass a sleepless night if they will study what is promised for their neglect to find the flock of his pasture by the various prophets.

In the 34th chapter of Ezekiel there is a solemn indictment of the shepherds of Israel (and I figure that these pastors of ours are the shepherds referred to) who have not sought for the lost sheep, but who have trod down the pastures and fouled the water provided for God's flock by their clouded reasoning and higher criticism. Read in the 31st verse who the flock are: "And ye, my flock, the flock of my pasture, are men and I am your God, saith the Lord God."

Who is so blind as Israel to-day—the Anglo-Saxon Celts? When Americans realize their identity and their inheritance, there will sure be some rattling of dry bones in their section of Israel or I miss my guess.

Man is naturally a religious animal and given religious propositions that he can see or reason out and put together in a reasonable way, he responds quickly. I know it, because I've "tried it on the dog," so to speak, with many of my business associates and friends. True you will meet an occasional friend who seems to think he knows more about the Bible than the Creator, and when you express a belief in the Bible as a true history, he will trot out some threadbare old question like "Do you believe the whale swallowed Jonah?" I never had any difficulty in believing that a Creator who could raise the dead, feed the children of Israel in the wilderness, and run this universe, could preserve Jonah in a live whale. The trouble is many men wish to size up the Creator as beieng in about *their* category as far as achievement is concerned!

I believe in the divine inspiration of Old and New Testaments and furthermore that days and dates set down therein have been *proved* to be correct, as checked by astronomical time. I have before me ten charts of chronology without a broken link from Adam to Christ. The author, Daniel Parker, of Lightcliffe, Halifax, England, spent fifteen years searching the Scriptures and other histories and says "In my life's history of researches I have found no history equal the splendid Chronological History [His-Story,— God's story] of the Bible, all of which is in accord with astronomical time and the literal fulfilment of God's covenants to His People, Israel." I have used Mr. Parker's work for the dates herein.

Now keep it fixed in your head that you, Brother Jonathan, are just as much a part of God's Israel as is Brother John Bull & Co., and that Brother Jonathan is the eldest son of Joseph and that Jacob passed to both these lads, Ephraim (England) and Manasseh (U. S. A.) the wonderful Joseph's blessings.

Read Moses' speech to Israel, Deuteronomy 33:4: "Moses commanded us a law." What sort of a law? "Even the inheritance of the congregation of Jacob." Who were the congregation of Jacob? They were Jacob's seed, Israel, who were gathered or congregated there, thus named after Jacob had wrestled with the angel and had so become a Prince of God or "ruling with God" as Young's Concordance has it, which is the meaning of his new name, Israel. What was the inheritance that was to be a law for them? The American and British portion, Moses' blessing of Joseph, is found in Deuteronomy 33:13-17. This included many blessings which we may enumerate as follows:

'Blessed of the Lord be his land
For the precious things of heaven
For the dew and
For the deep that coucheth beneath

And for the precious fruits brought forth by the sun

And for the precious things put forth by the moon

And for the chief things of the ancient mountains

And for the precious things of the lasting hills

And for the precious things of the earth and fulness thereof

And for the good will of him that dwelt in the bush.'

The record continues:

"Let the blessings come upon the head of Joseph, and *upon the top of the head of him that was separated from his brethren.* His glory is like the firstling of his bullock, and his horns are like the horns of unicorns: with them he shall push the people together to the ends of the earth: and they are the ten thousands of Ephriam, and they are the thousands of Manasseh."

You know how John Bull got his name when he marched with Moses under the bull or Engle flag and then bequeathed it to his country, Engle-land. You will have noticed his coat of arms: a lion and a unicorn, rampant, standing on a scroll, on which are the words *"Dieu et mon droit"*—God and my right. *What* right? My birthright—see I Chronicles 5:2: "But the birthright was Joseph's." The lion and unicorn are supporting a shield and on this shield are the words, *"Honi soit qui mal y pense"*—shamed be he who thinks evil of it.

"Israel ["ruling with God"] then shall dwell in safety alone"—as they have in the British Isles. "The foundation of Jacob shall be upon a land of corn and wine; also his heavens shall drop down dew." The lands and gardens of Britain, are lands of corn and wine, and has the dew that keeps its pastures as none other in the world that I have ever seen.

> "Happy art thou, Oh Israel: who is like unto thee, O people saved by the Lord, the shield of thy help, and who is the sword of thy excellency! and thine enemies shall be found liars unto thee; and thou shalt tread upon their high places" (vs. 29)—and we have!

Ferrar Fenton's translation into modern English from the original Hebrew for verses 28 and 29 reads:

> "Israel dwells alone, and secure,
> Jacob's spring in a land of the corn and fruit,
> And his skies will drop down dew!
> Blest Israel! who is like you?
> A Victor Race for Jehovah,—
> Your shield, your help, and your sword!
> You shall grow, and subdue your foes,
> And advance on their hills like a road."

The British fill every item of the above specifications and Americans were and still are Brith-ish i.e., Covenant men, as I will prove later.

THE DESTINY OF AMERICA

We Anglo-Saxons have been a victor race, and Jehovah has been our help, our shield, and our sword; Israel have always subdued their foes. Our enemies, both open and secret, have been found liars whose words were full of deceit and whose written engagements have been scraps of paper; and this applies to more than Germany.

You will note in verse 17 that the work of Joseph's descendants was to push the people *together,* not apart, to the ends of the earth, and both Britain and the United States have been on that job for hundreds of years. They have both worked for the unity of peoples. Take India where there are sixteen nations or sections and all religions; we are keeping the peace there and have tried to bring peace, law, order and justice to all nations they came in touch with or who were under their influence, the world over.

Manasseh (U.S.A.) means *forgetfulness* and it would seem as if America had forgotten the inheritance promised them which was to be a law to them and their Brother John for ever, though they have provided the melting pot for all nations, languages and religions in their little red school house where one language for all is taught and that is the language of the Covenant people.

DETAILS OF CHAPTER VI.

1. Every Bible prophecy has or will come to pass at its ordained time.
2. What nations have God's gifts promised to Joseph's seed.
3. Only America, Great Britain and Anglo-Saxon Celtic nations can qualify.
4. Moses, Hebrew leader of Israel, promised the wealth of the ancient hills to God's people, national Israel of Joseph's seed.
5. If the Creator's material promises made for this earth come true, then we are certain that the spiritual and heavenly promises will likewise come true.
6. Abraham Lincoln, man of God and leader in Israel, said "God has given America the four fundamental blessings" and these were promised by Moses to Joseph's seed.
7. Charles M. Schwab, a modern leader in Israel (American section) said, God has given America just the blessings Moses promised to Israel.
8. Has America the chief things of the ancient hills? She sure has!
9. Who has the oil supplies of the world?
10. How Britain is always paid for her missionary work.

THE DESTINY OF AMERICA

11. Mr. Joseph Daniels, Secretary of the Navy, on oil.
12. Why he should not get "Het Up" or lose sleep over it.
13. God set the bounds of America in Adam's time.
14. Jehovah saw that her cellars were filled with coal, oil, iron, copper, silver and gold.
15. Jehovah used the lure of gold with the 49'rs to people the West.
16. When His Royal Highness the Prince of Wales landed in New York.
17. Our Prince is decended from David, King of Israel. The proof is in Windsor Castle and another in the College of Heraldry in London awaiting your Ambassador's inspection.
18. The Prince of Wales is Prince of the House of Israel.
19. Why Americans are as much Brith-ish (Covenant Men) as are Englishmen, Canadians or Australians.
20. Britons 200 B.C. made an attractive headachy drink.

CHAPTER VI.

Now, if you believe in the inspiration of our Bible, you will understand from Moses' speech in the previous chapter that somewhere on this round earth are a people who have the choicest inheritance ever bequeathed to men, and further, there was no time limit mentioned when this unlimited inheritance would not be in force.

Every prophecy in the Bible inspired by God has come to pass, or it must and will, in its proper and ordained time. Moses' correct estimate of the character of Joseph and his knowledge of divine law enabled him to foresee the great prosperity which was bound to come to the children of Joseph, and he knew that his words were to be fulfilled in the same way that Jesus knew, when he said, "Heaven and earth shall pass away, but my words shall not pass away." Christ came not to do away with the law but to fulfil the law and the prophets.

If you were asked to-day, "Where are the nations who have the choicest blessings ever vouchsafed to mankind and what nations have carried God's blessing of peace as laid down by Moses?" who would you say had them? Would

THE DESTINY OF AMERICA

you say that our splendid ally, France, had inherited them when she has been overrun time after time throughout the ages?—as when she had her Reign of Terror and when she was bled white by Napoleon, etc., etc.? Would you say it was Russia that enjoyed all the good things of this earth while she was ground under by the Czars for centuries and to-day groans under a more diabolical regime than ever before afflicted her people? Is it Poland, dismembered for centuries? Is it Austria-Hungry, the ramshackle empire now reaping the fruits of her years of subservience to Germany? Is it Italy, overrun by invaders century after century? Is it Spain, Bulgaria, Servia, Greece, Turkey or Iceland? Is it Africa or China that fill these specifications by having God's choicest gifts bestowed upon them as nations? Any intelligent man can verify prophecies of the Bible by histories written hundreds and thousands of years since these promises were made by Moses, and can see that, of all the citizens of this round earth, to one people and only one do these blessings of Jehovah apply,—namely, to the Anglo-Saxon commonwealths or nations of which the United States of America is such a large factor.

If any of your great-grandfathers had bequeathed you the wealth of a small portion of the everlasting hills now controlled by, say, the Guggenheimers, you would, I imagine, be scratching gravel until you could establish your descent from the aforementioned great-grandfather. Well, the Guggenheimers have not the billionth part of America's national estate bequeathed to the eldest son of Joseph and his heirs as depicted in the 33rd chapter of Deuteronomy. You were to have an immense assortment of wealth: your land was to be blessed in everyway and *you do not have to die to obtain it;* you get it right on earth, as it is the visible tangible wealth that your banks lend money upon. Surely America has in her portion the wealth of the dew and rain; the wealth of the precious fruits brought forth by the sun and the moon; the wealth of fertile fields and valleys; the wealth of coal fields, oil fields, copper, silver, gold and the blessings of peaceful work.

As a parcel is tied with a cord, so are the tribes of Israel. Jacob is the cord that ties together God's inheritance, according to Deuteronomy 32:9: "For the Lord's portion is his people; Jacob is the lot (marg. "cord") of his inheritance."

When Germany and her partners in sin, seen and unseen, "the house of the evildoers" that "work iniquity," set out to break the cord of understanding and goodwill that binds all Anglo-Saxondom together, what was the result? Just what the Psalmist said (Ps. 2:2-4):

> 2. "The kings of the earth set themselves, and the rulers take counsel together [Germany, Austria,

THE DESTINY OF AMERICA

Turkey], against the Lord, and against his anointed [Israel], saying,

3. "Let us break their bands asunder, and cast away their cords from us.

4. "He that sitteth in the heavens shall laugh: the Lord shall have them in derision."

Were they held in derision by the Creator? It certainly looks like it. Germany lost all those waste places of the earth that she had spent years and billions of marks in building up, besides losing Alsace and Loraine, etc., etc. Her co-partner, the ramshackle empire, is dismembered and dying. Turkey has lost about everything she held dear, Mecca, Jerusalem and Constantinople.

Did they break the bands of the Lord's anointed (Israel)? Well, not that you would notice! Ask of that young Prince of Israel, David, Edward, Prince of Wales, if the bands of the Empire were broken asunder by the assaults of the "evildoers" who "work iniquity." Rather has the war brought to the attention of all who speak the English tongue the fact that if the world is to be saved from anarchy, they, with God's help, are the only peoples who can accomplish such a stupendous task.

I am willing to stake my reputation as a business man on Moses' blessing pronounced upon Joseph's descendants, the American and British sections of Israel.

If we find that the Bible promises of over three thousand years ago about the material things we were to receive on this earth have been fulfilled, then one may fairly deduce that those spiritual promises not yet fulfilled on this earth and to be fulfilled hereafter must certainly come true. Is that not a reasonable deduction? Do these fulfillments not prove that the Bible *is the inspired book it professes to be?*—because three thousand years is a long stretch to look ahead and forecast a great people's material prosperity. Leastwise it seems so to my way of thinking.

Note that Israel was to be set on high above all the nations of the earth.

> "And Moses and the priests the Levites spake unto all Israel, saying, Take heed, and hearken, O Israel; this day thou art become the people of the Lord thy God. . . . The Lord thy God will set thee [Israel] on high above all nations of the earth." (Deut. 27:9; 28:1.)

This you see was not a church set on high, but was a nation to be set above all other nations. Where, I ask, is that nation to-day that is set on high above all others? Has the promise failed? Just read through the promises made to all Israel in the foregoing two chapters and the punishments they were to receive for not obeying His commandments. They have indeed come true as the ages have rolled round.

See Deuteronomy 30:1-3; and it won't hurt you, even unaccustomed as you may be to Bible reading, to read right through to Chapter 33:13,

WHO OWNS THE COAL SUPPLIES OF THE WORLD?
This represents the present coal output.

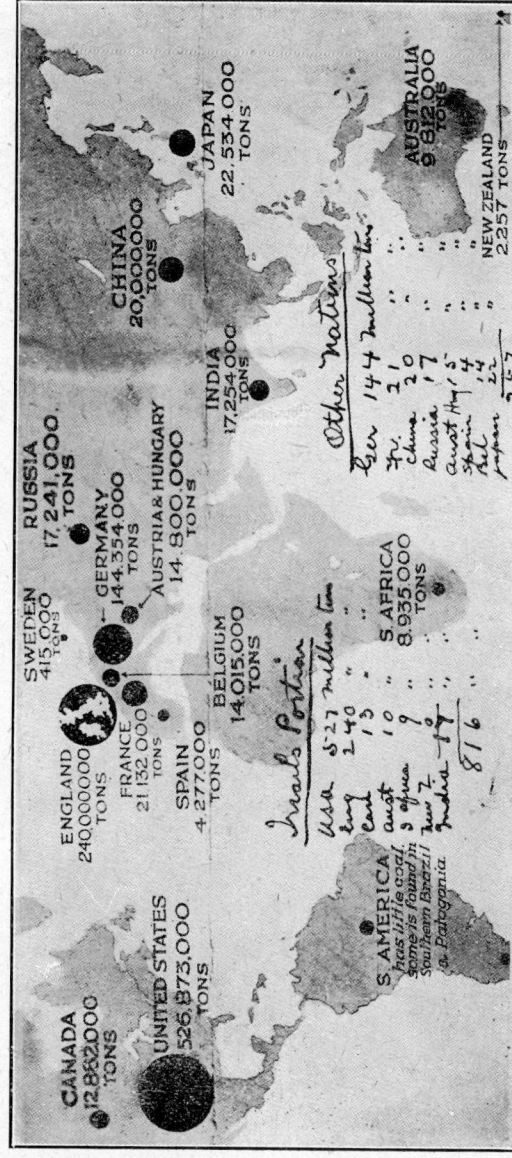

God promised Joseph the wealth of the ancient hills and the deep that coucheth beneath. The seed of Joseph's two sons, Manasseh (U.S.A.), Ephraim (Eng.), have received the lion's share.

where Moses prophesied the benefits coming to the descendants of your forefather and first food controller, Joseph, to you who are his seed.

Has America received the blessings of the Lord and the "precious things of heaven"? They have received God's laws and ordered liberty with the largest measure of peace of any nation and have been blessed from their earliest beginning— I can hear you murmur, "Yes, they have," even at this distance.

Has America received the blessings of the "dew" and the "deep that coucheth beneath [the springs and water tables below]"? No country has been more blessed with the dew, the rain and the deep that coucheth beneath. An American famine for lack of these things has been unknown in your history while other nations have not been so blessed.

Has America been blessed "for the precious fruits brought forth by the sun, and for the precious things put forth by the moon"? Why certainly they have. You are shipping your surplus bananas, Oregon apples, California prunes, olives, and raisins, Florida and California oranges and lemons all over the earth, and your Maine potato crops are known the continent over, while your corn is the wonder of the world, not to mention your wheat, oats, rye, etc.

And "for the chief things of the ancient mountains, and for the precious things of the lasting hills''? Well you have them! A glance at the maps opp. pp. 114-115 shows where we get off on oil in the coming fuel age, and for an essential like coal, a glance at the map shows that Brother John and Brother Jonathan have the lion's share. Take nickle; I am told that 95 per cent. of the world's supply comes from Canada to New York. Take copper; America absolutely produces and controls the world output. Take zinc; take almost anything; and it is the same story. Take a key essential like steel. "The United States Steel Corporation alone with a capital of $575,000,000 makes more steel than all Europe and they are only one of the many steel companies doing business in America"*—given to Joseph's seed for an inheritance.

Never having had the pleasure of meeting that master mind of the world on steel production, Charles M. Schwab, I am unable to say whether he is a student of Bible prophecy or not, but I should judge the chances rather favor the "not," therefore he probably may not know that Joseph's offspring were promised the wealth of the ancient hills and mountains. However, on January 5th, 1921, at the Copley Plaza in Boston, Mr. Schwab before the Massachusetts Bankers' Association made the following statement of fact*: *"Our United States has been endowed by God with*

---

*Boston *News Bureau*, Jan., 1921,

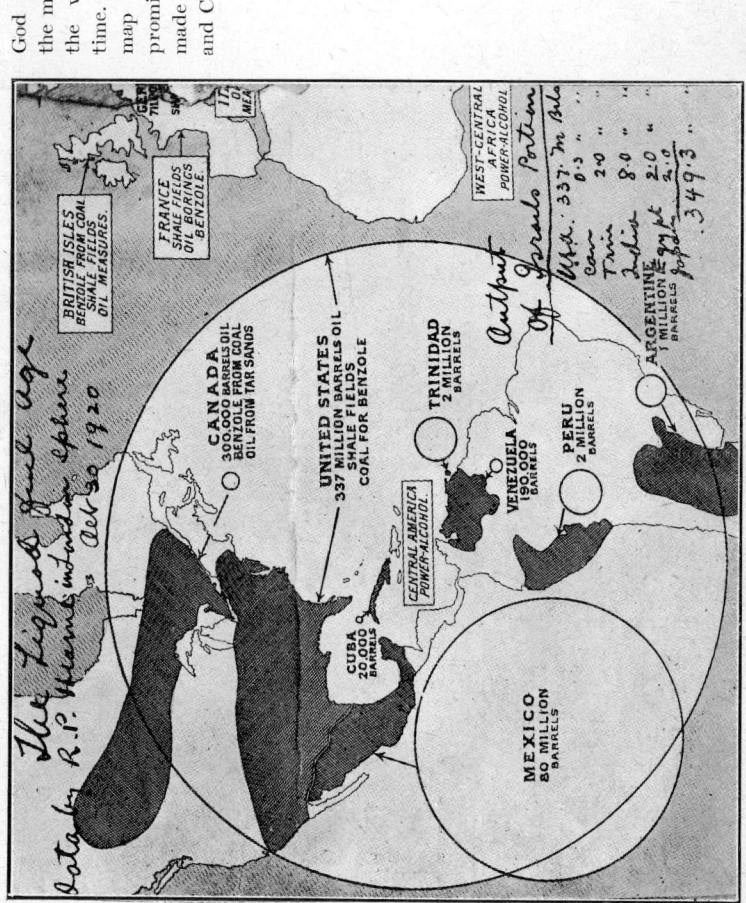

God promised Israel the material wealth of the world in Moses' time. A glance at the map shows how this promise has been made good to U. S. A. and Canada in oil.

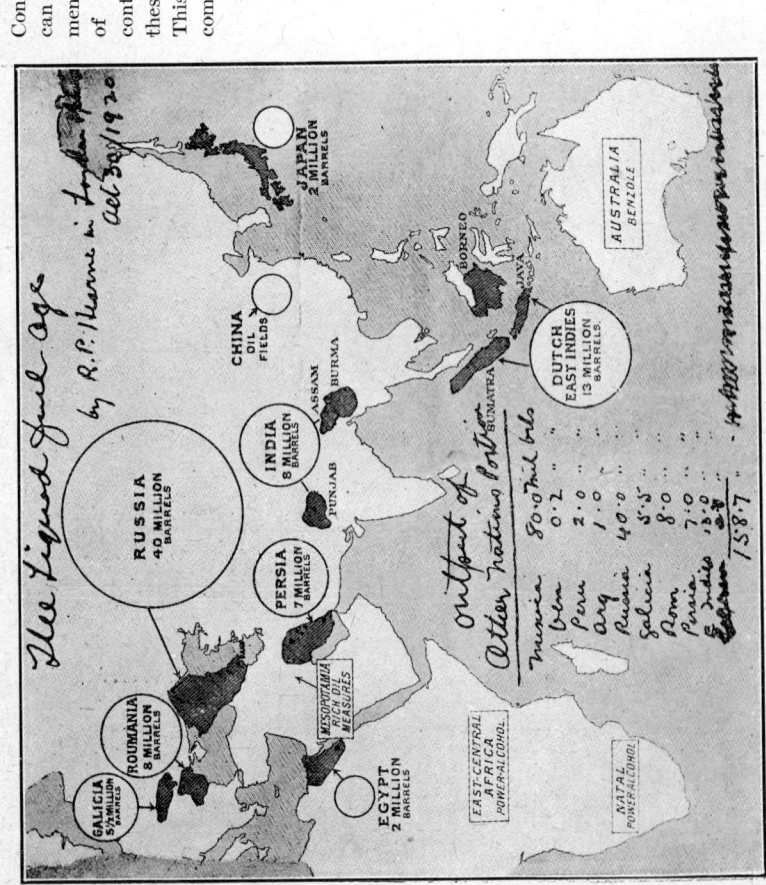

Contrast with American map and remember that citizens of Israel own and control the most of these supplies of oil. This prophecy has come true!

THE DESTINY OF AMERICA

everything to make it and keep it the foremost Industrial and Commercial Nation of the world.''

Charles M. Schwab says that America has everything necessary to keep it in front of the whole world, and that it was endowed by God with it; and that is exactly what Moses prophesied for the house of Joseph. Gentlemen, I rest my case there. If you know of any better authority on prophecy than the Bible or any better authority than Charles M. Schwab on prosperity or on the material possessions of America, just trot them out.

Abraham Lincoln at twenty-six years of age sensed God's goodness to *His servant Israel in America.* "He was firm in the belief that God was at the helm, and that man was but the humble though co-operating agent through whom the Almighty was working out the destiny of mankind."*

In a speech before the Young Mens' Lyceum of Springfield, Illinois, at about that age, he said: "We find ourselves in the peaceful possession of [1] the fairest portion of the earth, [2] as regards fertility of soil, [3] extent of territory, and [4] salubrity of climate. . . . We . . . . find ourselves the legal inheritors of these fundamental blessings. We toiled not in the acquirement or the establishment of them."*

---

*Abraham Lincoln Man of God, by John Wesley Hill.

"As Lincoln journeyed from Illinois across the country," Mr. Hill writes, "he declared all along the route that he was going forth in the name of the Living God of Israel."*

Well, reader, the point here is that if Lincoln knew that he was going forth "in the name of the Living God of Israel" and he could recognize the source of America's blessings, there is no reason why you need be ashamed to see it and to acknowledge it.

America has in full measure the very things promised to Ephraim and Manasseh,—brothers in 1713 B.C. as they are to-day,—Brother John and Brother Jonathan.

It is noted that the sphere sketch does not show any oil in Abyssinia, formerly called Ethiopia in Bible times. I had a commander of the Royal Navy at my home recently and was telling him how it was Britain's and America's job to settle the waste places of the earth and they would receive payment therefore by gettting the wealth of the everlasting hills and of the deep below the earth.

He was a Scot, a canny Scot, a man of few words. I had been telling him that Abyssinia would be against us in the great battle of Armageddon, though I had noticed in September, 1919, I think it was, that the British had given the Mad

---
*Abraham Lincoln Man of God, by John Wesley Hill.

Mullah a bad licking with aeroplane and machine guns.

"Man," says he, "we have been policing it and pouring in millions of money there year after year and I often wondered why we did it, as the bally place was no use to us."

Well, sir, as a result of the last licking we gave the Mad Mullah, we have found more oil in Abyssinia than there is in all Persia. So, again Mother Britain is repaid for policing and maintaining order, law and justice in these waste places of the earth that were to be your inheritance as well as hers.

> "Ask of me, and I shall give thee [Israel] the heathen for thine inheritance, and the uttermost parts of the earth for thy possession." (Ps. 2:8.)

Both Britain and America have made good the prophet's words and promises. Strange, but this new find is just where Britain will need it for going into the Suez Canal from the South, also the American Navy and Merchant Marine, which by that time will perhaps all be equipped with oil-burning apparatus.

I notice in this morning's paper, December 28, 1920, that your Secretary of the Navy, Mr. Josephus Daniels, has a belief that your government should prohibit the use of all fuel oil save for ships, and he proposes a brand new policy for the United States.

"I am in favor of the nationalization of coal, oil and water-power wealth of the nation. The statesmanship of our day should redeem the folly of earlier days," he says, "when these prime necessities were left unregulated to our lasting injury." What a pity our politicians, as well as yours, chuck out stuff like this *when leaving office* instead of bringing it about while they are in office! It would have been a feather in Mr. Daniel's cap if, when war was declared, he had taken the Standard Oil and the other oil refiners by the scruff of the neck and the seat of their pants and said, "Now, you chaps must work for Uncle Sam for a dollar ten per day, just like our fighting men at the Front. We will take your output at cost plus 10 per cent." America then would have saved enough to help pay her share of the war, instead of bulging out the already overfilled pockets of the oil magnates. President Harding has served notice that conscription will be for all in America's next big war, plants as well as men and he does well.

I had not noticed that Secretary Daniels was particularly keen along these lines during his turn at the wheel, but then I was very busy at the Front and may have overlooked some things. I don't suppose it would be any use for an ordinary dock-wholloper like myself to tender an old sea-dog, like Mr. Daniels, any advice on fuel for ships. But I would like to say to the Secretary,

THE DESTINY OF AMERICA

"Mr. Daniels, if I were you, I wouldn't get all het up worrying over the fuel supply for your big navy. It's just possible that the Creator fixed it all up for America when this world was put on its turning points and that he saw to it that your cellars had a good stock of coal, oil, copper, silver, gold, etc., because, 'When the Most High divided to the nations their inheritance, when he separated the sons of Adam, he set the bounds of the people according to the number of the children of Israel.'"

You will note that God had a plan for this universe in Adam's time, which was before there was a U. S. Navy, long, long before there were any children of Israel. And as the bounds of the nations were set then so the United States of America was provided for and as the descendants of Manasseh were to become a "great people," as the prophets foretold, they would need plenty of elbow room, plenty of coal, plenty of oil, plenty of iron and other necessities; for they were to take in all peoples and become the melting pot of all nations who would obey America's laws and *so become Israelites by adoption and by their belief in Christ.*

In comparatively a few years the King of Israel, whose right it is, will come to His Kingdom to see what his ten servants (the 10 tribes) have done during his absence with the talents he gave them when he commissioned them to *Oc-*

cupy until I come. What will America's answer be in those days if asked why they ducked their share of the white man's burden in Armenia in 1919 or 1920? America must stick by the commission. "Go ye into all the world" and not live for America alone.

When your country was settled only on the East and South, the lure of the gold in California's ancient hills drew your citizens across the great wilderness that then was between the East and the West; and so while giving them the wealth it also succeeded in peopling all America from East to West with an hundred and ten million intelligent prospective Israelites, and more coming. As Ephraim was promised the crown for David's seed, America had to be satisfied with a republic, and you are. But day and night are still doing business with us and so is God's Covenant, and somewhere ruling to-day over Israel is the seed of David, his servant—if not in Brith-ain, where is it?

I happened in New York City in 1919 and called on my early chief down at Battery Place the morning our Prince of Wales landed on the Battery steps, where his grandfather had landed some sixty years before. America took that young Prince to its heart in a way that could not have been more real, true, and lasting, if he had been their own Prince.

New York honored itself and did honor to as fine a young man as ever stepped in army shoe-leather that morning. We Canadians are proud of him and of his work, and it warmed the cockles of my heart to see that you were proud of our Prince, the Prince of the House of Israel. I somehow wished that morning that he might fall in love with an American beauty of the old covenant stock who might become his Better Half and so join the two sections of Israel ("ruling with God") together even more closely than they are now, because to-day there is a world-wide conspiracy to drive these brothers apart that must and will meet defeat.

The Prince's motto is "I serve"; and many times I passed him beating it alone and on foot along the railway tracks near an R. E. park called "Ondank Siding" on his way up to the Front of the 14th Corps to which he was attached during the terrific Paschendale fighting in front of Ypres in 1917. Having an extra star on my tunic above what he wore, the Prince always saluted it as I passed him, as if I were the King of England and he the Roadbuilder, a lesson in true democracy to those who serve.

When the Prince stayed with the Canadian Corps at the Front, he showed himself as true a democrat as ever grew on America's verdant soil. It is customary in any army mess at evening dinner for all to remain seated until the senior officer rises. The Chief in this case was Lieutenant-General, Sir Arthur Currie, who before the war was a real estate agent in Vancouver, B.C. and a major in the local volunteers, and who won his promotion at the Front step by step by sheer merit and hard work from the earliest days of the war. The Prince was the latest arrival at the mess and the evening he arrived when General Currie rose to leave the table, the Prince lived up to his motto of "I serve" by going to the door and opening it for the corps commander and the senior officers to pass out while he stood at attention. It was a delightful touch, and its spontaneity showed the true heart and instinct beneath his khaki tunic.

America, when she knows it, is as much a part of the House of Israel as is Canada, Australia or New Zealand and I have a feeling before many years you chaps living below the 49th parallel will be glad to think and to know that you nationally are of the House of Israel.

The British Isles were visited by Pytheas, a Greek navigator who sailed around Britain in the third century B.C. and reported that in those days they made an attractive drink "Kurmi" which gave one a pain in the head and also affected one's nerves (both, presumably the morning after).* So times have not changed much along some lines during 2200 years.

---

*Lecture on Britain, by Sir Bertram Windle.

When the Romans invaded Britain, these Brythons were in possession of a gold coinage, were manufacturers of beautifully wrought shields of bronz and enamelled ornaments and were not the naked skin-clad barbarians depicted in some histories. They had a civilization far in advance of Rome of that time. They carried Christianity from the Isles and planted it firmly in Rome itself through and by means of their royal family when the British Christian King Caradoc or Caractacus being defeated was taken there as a prisoner together with his son Linus and his daughters. St. Paul, in his second Timothy 4:21, sends greetings to this early Welsh Christian whose home was a meeting place for the Apostles and all Christians. The first Bishop of Rome was a Welshman, the Welsh Prince Linus. This is stated by Clemens Romanus who became the third Bishop of Rome only thirteen years after. It is also proved by the unimpeachable Irenaeus, of the second century: "The blessed Apostles having formed and built up the church, put into the hands of *Linus* the ministry of the Episcopate. These facts and many others just as interesting are proved in a little book by George Howard-Wright, M.A.—*Glastonbury our Mother* (price 1 shilling), and also by Rev. R. W. Morgan's *St. Paul in Britain or the Origin of British Christianity*.

CHAPTER VII.

1. Sky pilots in our mess.
2. My first cousin, Major Blank, the Jew.
3. I foretell we will win the Holy Land and give it to the Jews for a national home.
4. What Arthur J. Balfour, Secretary of State, did not know.
5. Why the Jews have to go back to Palestine representatively.
6. Why Arthur J. Balfour had to turn a somersault and eat his own words within a few weeks of uttering them.
7. Sir Herbert Samuels, Ephraim Israel's representative in Palestine, representing King George V.
8. Why the tribe of Benjamin was left with the Jews for some years.
9. Why God divided what had been the joint kingdom of Judah and Israel.
10. This, the key of all prophecy concerning Israel, is not understood by the churches. Why?
11. Why Benjamin was to be a light to lighten the world.
12. Why America was to be partially blind to their origin until Britain chased the Turk out of Jerusalem.

13. Where your forefathers first said "We are a great people."
14. Canadians and Americans at the Front always brothers.
15. Our Lord took God's Kingdom from the Jews and gave it to a nation.
16. To an enduring nation who would bring forth the fruits thereof it was to endure for a thousand generations, as the sun and moon it was to be daily and nightly before us. Where is that nation to-day? There are not many to pick from!

CHAPTER VII.

One evening we were dining in our mess, located in a small village behind Bethune, during March, 1917. We had an old chateau to ourselves, barring a dozen families of chimney martins that shared the hallways with us, there being no windows to keep them out. Each nest later had four wide-eyed young ones in it with their heads out over the edge as we went to and fro.

As will happen when ten or twelve men eat several meals a day together for almost 365 days of the year, talk languished.

We had two Sky Pilots with us as a regular diet and they favored us with many visiting clergymen with such glorious appetites! Why are parsons always so hungry, I wonder. It always seemed as if it was my luck to foregather with from one to three of them in each mess I got into, until I grew to think that some one in authority thought I was in special need of the daily and personal attention from them or else they desired to have the Padres' vocabularies enlarged along certain explosive lines very necessary in driving army mules, of both varieties—two legged and four legged!

Well, this evening conversation languished, and to make talk, I chucked out something about the Jews to my clerical friends across the table.

The good-looking young major sitting next to me on the right gently tapped me on the knee under the table and whispered,

"You know, Major Blank is a Jew."

Major Blank sat next to me on my left. Of course I knew he was a Jew, as did everyone else, because he had a typical Jew nose and face, and the Jews' business capacity. I replied out loud,

"Of course I know Major Blank is a Jew; he is a first cousin of mine! The Major belongs to the tribe of Levi or Judah, while I am from the tribe of Benjamin on my mother's side and from the tribe of Gad on my father's side."

Turning to the Major I said, "By the way, Major, I suppose you remember that the Bible said of your tribe of Judah (Isaiah 3:9): 'The shew of their countenance doth witness against them'? And so down through the ages you can always tell a Jew as far away as you can see his face."

"You know, Major," I continued, "we are going to win Jerusalem, Palestine, and the Holy Land back from Turkey (or Edom, as the Bible refers to it) as predicted in the single chapter of Obadiah, and we are going to give it to you chaps for a national home for Jews under Great Britain."

But, the Major wouldn't have any! In the first place he didn't believe the Bible was inspired; 'twas just Hebrew symbolical literature, and in the second place the Jews didn't want Jerusalem and wouldn't go back if they had it.

"Well, Major, you ought to be an authority on Jews, but I'm sure you will pardon me if I prefer the authority that has been proved correct, in hundreds of predictions extending down through the ages, as to the persecution, etc., the Jews were to receive for their actions and for having rejected and crucified our Lord. 'His blood be on us and our children,' they cried, and for nineteen hundred years it certainly has been, and they got what they asked for all right. If you take the Bible prophecies about Judah and the Jews in Isaiah, first five chapters, and then read history you will see that each Bible prophecy or prediction due up to date has come true. Therefore you might expect the prediction that they were to be joined to the house of Israel on the hills of Palestine, after Ephraim Israel had cleaned out the Turk, to come true"—as it has to the very letter, both to Judah (the Jews) and to Ephraim Israel (Britain).

"The Bible says, Major, that you hooked-nosed chaps are going to hike back to Palestine representatively, one of a city and two of a family. There will be two Cohens, two Abrahams, two Leons, two Moses, etc."

Nothing doing for the Major, 'twas all bunk! But this is what we read in Jeremiah

THE DESTINY OF AMERICA

3:14, "And I will take you one of a city, and two of a family, and I will bring you to Zion"—or the Holy Land.

However, General Allenby, that most sympathetic of all our army commanders, happily selected for that job, finally won Jerusalem; and immediately the Zionist societies of Britain and elsewhere set up a holler for a national home for the Jews. But Arthur J. Balfour, then Secretary of State for Foreign Affairs, turned them down flat—nothing doing.

The Major met me at breakfast the morning the London *Times* reached us with this news.

"Well sir," says he, "you don't get your national home for Jews in Palestine."

"You bet your last pair of socks we will," says I.

"Why? Didn't you see what Balfour said?"

"Sure I did, but that doesn't cut any ice," says I. "Britain's ministers and prime ministers have had to eat their words dozens of times within my recollection when they got off the track of the plan the Creator has laid down for Britain to follow. Take Gladstone's promise to get out of Egypt. Did he do it? Not on your life! Because he couldn't and he had to eat his words and promises time after time about that and other things. Balfour, Major, is a big toad in the British puddle and a charming man; but big as he is, he is not yet running the universe and I have it on the authority of the Runner of the Universe that both the Jews and Israel are going back to Jerusalem, representatively, and they will be under a king there, the descendant of King David of Israel, so Great Britain must have the mandate, as she has the only king who clearly is descended from King David of Israel and Jerusalem with an enduring dynasty—see Psalm 89.''

Well, inside a week or two Arthur J. Balfour had to turn one of those complete somersaults that our politicians find so necessary to execute at times when they get on the wrong side of the political fence, and working against the Creator's plan laid down in God's Word; and he agreed that Great Britain would use her best influence to try to bring about a national homeland for Jews in Palestine. France followed suit, then Italy, and I believe the United States did likewise.

After I got home from the Front in the spring of 1919 one of our daily papers gave an account of a conference of Zionist societies from the Western States which met in Chicago. They decided to send representatives to the Holy Land. And how did they select them? Why, just as the Bible said they would: "One of a city" to the number, I think it was, of 302 representatives. In the same paper was a cable from London that the Zion Society of Palestine had cabled the British Foreign Office not to allow over 50,000 Jews, I think it was, to return that year as they could not accommodate all that were flocking in—See Jer. 3:14: "And I will take you one of a city, and two of a family, and I will bring you a Zion."

I cut out both these clippings, enclosed them, and wrote a note to my first cousin (some removed), the Jew major, who, like myself, was a civilian, and asked: "How about the Creator knowing more about the Jews than you did?" After many moons the Major got the letter in that quaint old walled city of Lille and wrote me some months later saying he had been holding off until he saw the final outcome of the whole Palestine layout.

Sir Herbert Samuels, High Commissioner for Palestine, had left England for the Holy Land and a close relation of the Major's, who was a staunch Zionist, was one of Sir Herbert's staff advisers. The Major was very hearty in his congratulations on the predictions coming out exactly as had been stated, but he figured no Holy Land for his! He would sooner sell boots to the pilgrims enroute for there. I wrote and told him some of the particulars that were yet going to happen to that section of country that the Creator selected as the homeland for His selected seed, both Judah and Israel.

By the way, it was predicted Judah should walk with, or as the margin has it, "to" Israel; and they have been doing it by filling large sections of most every city in the United States,

Great Britain and Canada (all portions of Israel) with Jews at such an alarming rate during the last twenty-five years, and so much to the disgust of some pillars of Israel—that one of them wrote me recently from England he "wished to God they'd all go back to Palestine and stay there." Well, this particular pillar of Israel happens to be a somewhat peppery general who does not know that there are those "which say they are Jews, are not, but are the synagogue [or congregation] of Satan."

The Major, being an Englishman for many generations, was as stiff-necked as the average of that tribe about a new idea and would not have any joining of Britain (Ephraim Israel) with Judah until he saw it as an accomplished fact two years later. I might have quoted the prophets to him, but not being a believer in the Bible as inspired, he would have said it was "bunkum" and he would not have been able to see it; besides, he might have retorted by some reference to the "Devil quoting Scripture,"—as some of my messmates thought I was a pretty stout limb of Satan anyway. Such is reputation!

Look up Ezekiel 37:19-22.

19. "Say unto them, Thus saith the Lord God; Behold, I will take the stick of Joseph, which is in the hand of Ephraim [England], and the tribes of Israel his fellows—Simeon (the Welsh), Gad (Lowland Scotch), Benjamin (Normans), etc., etc.—and will

THE DESTINY OF AMERICA

put them with him, even with the stick of Judah, and make them one stick, and they shall be one in mine hand.

20. "And the sticks whereon thou writest shall be in thine hand before their eyes [before the eyes of all the world].

21. "And say unto them, Thus saith the Lord God; Behold, I will take the children of Israel from among the heathen, whither they be gone, and will gather them on every side, and bring them into their own land [Palestine—given to their forefather, Abraham].

22. "And I will make them one nation in the land upon the mountains of Israel; and one king shall be king to them all: and they shall be no more two nations, neither shall they be divided into two kingdoms and more at all."

Pretty strong medicine to hand out to an unbelieving Jew, eh what? I knew I'd have about as much chance of getting anywhere by quoting it to my friend the Major as a snowball has of becoming an icicle in the warm place, so I didn't trouble him with this data.

You may not know that *the Hebrew people were finally divided by the Creator into two nations about the year* 974 *B.C.* For hundreds of years they had been numbered and referred to separately even when under one king. Just here note that it is the lack of this knowledge and its application to Bible prophecies made about either Judah or Israel that is the cause of Churches' failure to properly grasp, interpret and see the prophecies concerning Israel's future and God's plan for her redemption after their dispersion by Shalmaneser, King of Assyria, and their being taken across the Euphrates.

You will see, in First Kings, Chapters 11 and 12, how these Hebrews were finally separated into two nations by God. King David had joined Judah and Israel together and ruled over them, yet note how in II Samuel 5:4, 5 Israel is mentioned separate from Judah:

> 4. "David was thirty years old when he began to reign, and he reigned forty years.
> 5. "In Hebron he reigned over Judah seven years and six months: and in Jerusalem he reigned thirty and three years over all Israel and Judah."

Solomon, David's son—born in 1033 B.C., crowned King of Israel in 1015, and died in 975 B.C.—was told that because of his idolatry and so forth (mostly so forth, as you will see by reading this interesting chapter), nine out of the ten tribes of Israel would be taken from his kingdom, not in his day but in his son's time.

> "And unto his [Solomon's] son will, I give one tribe, that David my servant may have a light alway before me in Jerusalem, the city which I have chosen me to put my name there." (I Kings 11:36.)

This was the tribe of Benjamin whom Moses blessed and said:

> "The beloved of the Lord shall dwell in safety by him; and the Lord shall cover him all the day long,

and he shall dwell between his shoulders." (Deut. 33:12.)

This tribe received Christ gladly when the Jews persecuted him. Eleven of the twelve apostles were Benjamites; the twelfth, Judas, a Jew, sold Jesus for thirty pieces of silver. The Jews would not receive Christ; but Benjamin, you will remember, was left temporarily with Judah when the kingdom was divided after the reign of Solomon, "that David my servant may have a light alway before me in Jerusalem." This Benjamin tribe received Christ and as His disciples started out to be the light to lighten the world, Jesus, instructing them, said: "Go not into the way of the Gentiles, and into any city of the Samaritans enter ye not: but *go rather to the lost sheep of the house of Israel*"—the sheep that had been taken captive. The sheep that had forsaken God and become idolaters had quit the Mosaic rites and laws and their first order to go to Israel rather than to Judah was afterwards amplified by a command to "go ye into all the world." Jesus knowing Israel was to be scattered among all the nations commanded his disciples to go into all the world.

When Rehoboam, King of Judah, with whom, as we said, were temporarily the tribe of Benjamin, numbering "an hundred and four score thousand chosen men, which were warriors," was making ready to fight against the House of Israel (who kicked over the traces because of the high taxes and heavy yokes, etc.—the sort of taxes their descendants to-day are complaining about in U.S.A.), "the word of God came unto Shemaiah, the man of God, saying, speak unto Rehoboam, the son of Solomon, king of Judah, and unto all the house of Judah and Benjamin, and to the remnant of the people, saying, Thus saith the Lord, Ye shall not go up, nor fight against your brethren, the children of Israel: return every man to his house; for this thing is from me. They hearkened therefore to the word of the Lord."

Now then, whether you believe in prophecy or not, history shews that Judah and Israel were divided and have been separate and distinct until, as foretold, they were joined together in Palestine after Edom or Turkey had been smashed in 1917. Just seven times (a time being 360 years) after it had fallen, i.e., 2520 years, and in the 2520 year General Allenby captured it and entered Jerusalem on foot, not as victorious troops but as a redeemer of the Holy Places.

If our clergyman could only see this division commanded to be made by God and would realize that when the Bible refers to Judah or the Jews, it means exactly what it says, since the

THE DESTINY OF AMERICA

<u>nation Israel (ruling with God) is as separate in prophecy from Judah as it is possible to make it,</u> they would get such new revelations that they would get us all to take out our disused Bibles and find the living Word of God more up to date than any publication in America or anywhere else.

Recently I heard one of the best educated Episcopal clergymen on this continent refer to St. Paul as "a little Jew." Now, St. Paul was as much "a little Jew" as I am "a little Newfoundlander" and no more! I telephoned this venerable gentleman and asked him why he called St. Paul "a little Jew."

"Well, he wasn't a Gentile was he?"—showing that he considered it necessary to be one or the other. St. Paul himself said in the 11th chapter of Romans, 1st verse:

> "I say then, Hath God cast away his people [Israel]? God forbid. For I also am an Israelite, of the seed of Abraham, of the tribe of Benjamin."

It is true his tribe was temporarily with the Judah Kingdom and he could say he was a Jew, temporarily, in the same way he could say he was a Roman citizen without stretching the truth, but, by birth he was of Israel and of the tribe of Benjamin, "beloved of the Lord," and he knew it, was proud of it and proclaimed it to the Jews and to Israel.

You will remember that the tribe of Benjamin was left with Judah, "that David, my servant, may have a light always before Me in Jerusalem." This light was to lighten the world and here was St. Paul who, together with Luke, Timothy and Mark in A.D. 61, carried this light to the British or Covenant Isles* where his brethren were. Read Romans 11: 25, 26, 30, where he was speaking to his own people, Israelites:

> 25. "For I would not, brethren, that ye should be ignorant of this mystery, lest ye should be wise in your own conceits; that blindness in part is happened to Israel, until the fulness of the Gentiles be come in."
> 26. And so all Israel shall be saved: as it is written, There shall come out of Sion the Deliverer, and shall turn away ungodliness from Jacob.
> 30. For as ye in times past have not believed God, yet have now obtained mercy through their unbelief.

Here you will notice that this partial blindness of Israel had a time limit. How long? "Until the fulness of the Gentiles be come in." Well, that time limit expired when the Holy City, Jerusalem, ceased to be trodden down by the infamous Ottoman, or O T'Heman, when Britain took possession by capture in 1917. This blindness in part is therefore now to be removed and it is just possible this screed may help along that line. Anyway, its up to Manasseh, the United

---

Far Hence unto the Gentiles, by Lumen (Major J. Samuels, V. D.).

THE DESTINY OF AMERICA

States section of Israel to get wise to the fact that they are that "great people" who in early days B.C. thumped their chests and hollered for more land because they were a great people, and they got it; since which time "though blinded in part," they have not entirely forgotten their chest-elevating habits, nor the inclination to holler "We are a great people." "We won the War!" "We will have the biggest navy afloat," etc. Bless your hearts, you can't help it any more than the rest of us. We, your neighbours on the North know you from your boots up. We know it is hard to live in the ozone-filled atmosphere of this North American Continent (of which don't forget we Canadians own the larger half) and not boast. We above the 49th parallel have our ardor a bit tempered by those gentle zephyrs wafting down from the Aurora Borealis area several months of the year; but even with this and among ourselves, there is a saying that a man cannot tell the truth about Canada anywhere west of Port Arthur. They just boast!

'Twas odd, but whenever we Canadians met a man from the U.S.A., whether officer or "Doughboy" at the Front, we felt 'twas someone from home. Motoring back from Germany in January, 1919, I passed through the American headquarters area at Coblenz, then into Treves where Marshall Foch has his headquarters. We went to the town major for a billet. I noticed he wore one of those straight corset-like, uncomfortable looking (for working) tunics of the U. S. Army, so I said.

"Hello, Yank! What are the chances for a shake-down for two officers and my chauffeur for the night?"

"Not very good, Sir," he replied, looking me over. "Where do you hail from when you are home?"

I told him. He knew my city. He was from Detroit (Park Davis Co.), and he dug us up a splendid billet, had my motor filled with gasoline and forgot to charge it, because our cities were not over a thousand miles apart, and because we told stories that each could understand without the aid of a mallet and chisel. We were brothers in ideas, in ideals, and in service.

We motored through beautiful old Luxembourg, Metz, Nancy and Verdun, Rheims, Noyen, Amiens and back to Lille. At Metz an American showed us the figure of the prophet Daniel, cut in stone, with the other prophets on the cathedral. Emperor William had had his own face, with its up-turned mustache, carved in place of the prophet Daniel's, but still retaining the latter's gown and folded arms! An Anglo-Saxon would have been tempted to smash it with an axe when they took over the city, but the French had a more subtle wit. They had a pair of large iron manacles made and placed on Daniel's folded arms, so

THE DESTINY OF AMERICA

there stands the Kaiser in irons on the corner of the Cathedral in Metz Public Square for future generations to admire!

At Verdun the only eating-place available was an American Y. M. C. A. in one of the semi-demolished buildings. 'Twas a cold, wet day and their roof was only a quarter left on and the balance badly splintered. My nose told me it was a Yankee chuck-house for I smelled flapjacks and maple syrup when I got inside the battered door. Noticing a vacant space on a plank alongside a young lady I hastily filled it, as women's company at the Front was a real treat.

"Well, Sister, what part of Yankee Land do you hail from?"

"Lincoln, Nebraska," says she as if with a clothes peg on her nose.

"Good gracious, but you're a long way from home aren't you? How did you make it?"

She was only about a handful and so frail-looking I wondered how she passed inspection.

"Is your billet dry?" I asked, seeing that she had a bad cold.

"Well, at times."

If the wind and rain blew from the west, they, she and another young lady, pushed their cots to the east side of the room where it was dry, but if it changed direction during the night their cots and blankets got wet. They gave us a bang-up hot meal, for we were chilled to the bone and they made us feel as much at home as if we were a William Jennings Bryan Jr. It was always thus when Americans and Canadians met: we were brothers in fact, as we are by inheritance and by that long distance relationship dating from our forefather as well as your forefather Joseph, the food controller in Egypt for those seven lean years 1700 B.C. to 1693 B.C.

When we realize the final division of the Hebrews into two separate nations as shown in this chapter, one is in a position to read intelligently future references, predictions and prophecies made concerning Israel as well as Judah throughout both the Old and New Testaments, and—if I may be pardoned for saying it (especially by the parsons, who, I find, dislike having a layman prod them or their Union when it comes to Bible facts)—no person can understand one half of the Old and New Testaments without this knowledge.

In Matthew 21: 43 Jesus speaking to the Jews said:

"Therefore say I unto you, the kingdom of God shall be taken from you [Jews], and given to a nation bringing forth the fruits thereof."

Many Episcopalian and other churchmen hold that God's Kingdom has been passed on to the church as custodians and they forget entirely the *"nation"* referred to by Jesus, a nation bringing forth the fruits thereof. Such a nation does exist to-day, who, with their offspring, are fulfilling every prophecy foretold about Israel; but the church is in no sense filling these prophecies. "There are none so blind as those who will not see!"—churchmen included!

Had I the time I would like to explore the churches' contention that they are Israel, as I could prove to your satisfaction that not one or even all the churches can qualify for this name since they are neither "a nation" nor do they properly bring forth "the fruits thereof." Their failure to properly bring forth the fruits as churches (not as nations) and carry forward the Creator's design therein caused to spring up those zealous Dissenters who in turn have not seen this truth except in spots,—Puritans, Baptists, Methodists and last but not least, that splendid host raised by that eminent Father in Israel, General Booth, for the further world-wide propagation of God's Word by deeds and works among those who need it most. I do not mention herein the Church of Scotland, offspring of the church Jeremiah founded in Ulster about the year 575 B.C., whose ministers (provided they were not educated at

Oxford) still largely believe the Bible is inspired from cover to cover.

I would not for a moment depreciate the good work done by the churches; but in my time they seem mostly in what the sailors would call the doldrums, sails all up ready for business but idly flapping from side to side. Since the German-made higher criticism fell by the wayside in 1914, they seem waiting for a breeze to carry them along towards their haven, and the congregations aboard are mostly busy dodging the boom as it idly flaps from side to side in the gentle roll of a calm undisturbed sea and getting nowhere. The breeze they need is in the Bible but their blind leaders spiritualize it away as the higher critics in Germany have done. They see the cross but fail to see the Crown or Kingship of National Israel the ten workmen Jesus told to "occupy" his kingdom until he comes to Earth to rule from Jerusalem.

I really have little license to criticize because I have never joined a church, though our parson, my children say, once referred to me from the pulpit "as a staunch pillar of the church," when I was in France—I wonder if he will withdraw it now! But being a religious animal I attended church regularly both at the Front, in England on leave, and at home, and I must confess that most churches seem to have a tendency to run to seed, side and formalism, without being especially hotbeds of brotherliness and light.

THE DESTINY OF AMERICA

They refuse to look through this window that God has opened for them in His inspired Word as if it was a man-made window and they bethump those who do as if they were infidels.

They seem to worship idols of Success, Glad Rags and New Bonnets quite as much as they do the Creator, and most of the ministers I have happened to hear, especially in England, reading the living Word of God make it about as attractive as is the reading of a dictionary of the last century.

As an alleged custodian and interpreter of God's Word given to men through the mouths of His prophets in our Old and New Testaments, every clergyman preaching from God's Word should be prepared to answer this question which I think a layman is entitled to ask.

What did Jesus mean by saying that the Kingdom of God would be taken from the Jews and given to a nation bringing forth the fruits thereof? Where is there such a nation? Where is the enduring throne of an enduring nation to be seen daily as the sun and moon are seen, as promised to David about 1024 B.C. in Psalm 89.

Is it Germany, Russia, Austria, or Turkey?
Is it Portugal, Italy, Spain or Ireland?
Methinks that only among the Anglo-Saxon nations can you find a people who,

even imperfectly, are still bringing forth the fruits of the Gospel our Lord taught when on earth.

The seed of David was to rule until Christ came again; therefore to-day, somewhere, there is reigning the seed of David.

Where are they? Who are the nations bringing forth the fruits of Bible teaching? What nations are spreading God's Word and laws broadcast over the earth?

Alfred, the Great, in his day placed the Ten Commandments at the beginning of British laws and further adopted many of Moses' national laws and statutes laid down for Israel in the Bible, and he did well. He also built the first national British navy. Psalm 89 says: "I will set his hand also in the sea, and his right hand in the rivers." Since the time of Alfred the Great Britannia, or Covenant of the sea, has ruled the waves and will now share it with Brother Jonathan, and perhaps Japan.

Who is doing the missionary work of the world to-day? Sir Walter Raleigh in 1588 gave £100 to the Virginia Company for the propagation of Christianity in that settlement, being the first recorded missionary work done in America; and it was done by a Covenant man— "Brith," Covenant and "ish," man.

Under Cromwell, in 1649, the Corporation for the Propagation of the Gospel in New England, new Bull land, was formed.

The United Kingdom of Great Britain and the United States of America are the two nations carrying on about 75 per cent. of the missionary work of the world as the following data will show, and whenever there is distress or famine or want the world over, the Anglo-Saxons give their substance, give heartily and give quickly, and give three times as much as all the rest of the world put together. Why, I wonder? This was foreseen by the prophets when we were given our world-wide commission.

The following figures just give you a faint idea of how Anglo-Saxons have been carrying on their job as missionaries to the heathen Gentiles and the demands for light and Bibles during the next few years will double and treble.

MISSIONARY WORK.

Work carried on in Asia, Africa, India, West Indies, China, Japan, Persia, Palestine, Central Asia, Brittany, Italy, Madagascar, South America and elsewhere by British Agencies.

British Missionary Society	When Organized	Number Stations	Male Missionaries	Female Missionaries	Native Helpers	Annual British Expenditure
Soc. for Propagation of Gospel	1701	4,520	520	186	5,200	£152,350
Moravians		379	200	194	1,864	21,606
Baptist Miss. Soc. and Gen'l. Baptist Soc.	1702	859	141	183	808	97,624
London Miss. Soc. (Congregational)	1795	1,357	210	239	6,462	145,271
Church Miss. Soc.	1799	590	571	757	8,106	252,161
C. of E. Tenna	1880	64	210	....	917	56,733
Wesleyan Meth.	1813	2,818	216	243	3,640	52,789
Ch. of Scotland	1829	84	50	82	855	41,967
United Free Scot.	....	827	99	207	2,813	108,309
Pres. Ch. of Ireland	1840	37	19	32	284	5,081
Pres. Ch. of England	1847	261	43	58	401	26,510
Welsh Calvanistic Meth.	1840	20	20	19	1,074	10,303
United Meth. Free Ch.	1857	193	26	22	584	12,647
Universities Miss. (Africa)	1859	....	69	48	207	30,371
Friends Foreign Miss.	1865	248	35	59	978	24,512
American Miss.	1844	54	38	33	46	5,746

and dozens of others.

There are about thirty thousand foreign missionaries in the field and only about 1,500 are of other nations than the Anglo-Saxon-Celts, though all who accept Christ as their Saviour are grafted into Israel and so become Abraham's seed.

CHAPTER VIII

1. Your Pilgrim Fathers, God-fearing men.
2. They believed they were Divinely lead in founding their Israel in the waste places in America.
3. God preserved the Pilgrim Vine which His own right hand had planted—they wrote.
4. The Pilgrims kept the Sabbath just as God said Israel would throughout their generations.
5. The book of Common Prayer is a book of common sense.
6. The Anglo-Saxon nations doing the missionary work which the Almighty said would be done by His servants Israel.
7. The waste places given to Israel to establish the earth.
8. In Europe, Asia, Africa, Australasia and America.
9. In Flanders' fields and America's reply.
10. The Ensign set up by the root of Jesse is the Union Jack or Jacob.
11. The first national flag of United States had the Union Jack or the Union of Jacob in the corner and was called the "Grand Union".
12. America's section of waste places.
13. America's Divine Commission was to take on with Brother John these waste places of the earth.

CHAPTER VIII.

Your Pilgrim Forefathers were a God-fearing body of men. "They entered into covenant to walk with God and one with one another, in the enjoyment of the Ordinances of God, according to the Primitive Pattern in the Word of God. But finding by experience they could not peaceably enjoy their own liberty in their Native Country, without offence to others that were differently minded, they took up thoughts of removing."*

They first went to Holland, and from there the spirit moved them to go to America. It took two years, however, before they could secure the right and a patent to take up land in Virginia. They had to explain that they were Englishmen and Protestants, that they assented to the doctrines of the Church of England and acknowledged the King's authority; and they *agreed not to become rebellious or dangerous colonists.* The government seemed to have a hunch even in that day that they were to lose America and so tied them to an agreement not to be rebellious, etc.

Chronicles of the Pilgrim Fathers with an Introduction by John Masefield, New York: E. P. Dutton & Co.

THE DESTINY OF AMERICA

After those in Holland had embarked and had stopped for their friends in England, the Pilgrims left Plymouth and started across the ocean in the "Mayflower" and the "Speedwell." On two occasions they had to sail back to England because of the unseaworthiness of the "Speedwell"; and they finally had to give up the "Speedwell," sell part of their provisions, and overcrowd the "Mayflower" when they made their final start, September 6-16, 1620, for Virginia.

The "Mayflower" had a tough passage, encountering many gales, in one of which her main beam was broken. But one of the Pilgrims had a jack screw and with this a repair was made and the voyage was continued. They made land November 9-19, 1620, at Cape Cod. The crew refused to sail down the coast in the teeth of the November gales, and the Pilgrims had to land and stay in Massachusetts though their patent was only for Virginia.

Right here may I mention how Providence guided these people and took care of them. Had they landed on any other section of the coast than where they did, they never could have survived the winter and the Indians. A plague had struck this section of country two years before and wiped out the Indians but left in a cave some eight bushels of Indian corn, which the Pilgrims used for seed for the season 1621, as they brought none from England.

On December 25th they commenced their first house. During that first winter they endured many hardships and lost their governor and one half the colony by death and the rest were so weakened that had the warlike Indians of the other parts of the coast been in this section of country, the Pilgrims could not possibly have survived.

In 1621 they secured a patent, granted by the English Council for New England (the new bull or Engle land).

Israel was to settle the coasts and waste places of the earth and drive the heathen before them. Was that promise fulfilled in the case of the Pilgrims when as Englishmen they settled New England? Can we do better than to take the words of the Pilgrims themselves? You can readily see that the heathen were driven out before them by the plague and the way made easy for them to build homes and become installed peacefully.

Nathaniel Morton, the historian addressed a Memorial to the Right Worshipful Thomas Prince, Governor of New England, published by E. P. Dutton & Co., N.Y., from which I have taken the following quotations:

"Have never seen nor heard of any [memorial writings] especially respecting this our plantation of

THE DESTINY OF AMERICA

New Plimouth, *which God hath honored to be the first in this land*, I have made bold to present your Worships with, and to publish to the world, something of the very first beginnings of *the great actions of God in New England, begun at New Plimouth*.

"I should gladly have spoken more particularly of the neighboring united colonies, whose ends and aims in their transplanting of themselves and families, were the same with ours, viz. *the glory of God, the propagation of the Gospel and enlargement of His Majesty's Dominions.* . . . .

"And declaration of God's wonderful works for, by, and to his People in preparing a place for them by driving out the Heathen before them . . and making this howling wilderness a chamber of rest, safety and pleasantness."

As early as 1623 these Englishmen kept days for fasting, humiliation, and prayer and in 1637 passed an ordinance: "That it be in the power of the governor and assistants to *command* solemn days of humiliation, and also for thanksgiving," and since then their American descendants have eaten the November Thanksgiving turkey and cranberry, with or without the aforementioned humiliation and prayer attachments and in many cases I'm afraid have forgotten what their predecessors knew in their souls, namely, that God had been and still was looking after them and "prospering their undertakings," as your Great Seal of State says, above the all-seeing eye.

Here are some paragraphs from *Chronicles of the Pilgrim Fathers* that is particularly appropriate to these times (when authority is looked askance by so many "Reds" and semi-"Reds," profiteers, etc.) and for electing representatives:

> "Lastly ... let your wisdom and godliness appear not only in choosing such persons as do entirely love, and will promote the common good; but also in yielding unto them all due Honor and Obedience in their lawful administrations, not beholding in them the ordinariness of their persons, but God's ordinance for your good; not being like the foolish multitude, who more honor the gay coat then either the virtuous mind of the man, or the glorious ordinance of God.
>
> "Ought not, and may not the children of these fathers rightly say, our fathers were Englishmen, which came over this great ocean, and were ready to perish in this wilderness, but they cried unto the Lord, and he heard their voice, and looked on their adversity."

About March 16, 1621, an Indian called Samoset came to the Puritan settlement. He could speak a little English and proved to be, they wrote, "a special instrument sent of God for their good, beyond expectation." He told them how to plant the corn they found left by the plague-killed Indians, where to fish for the fish so necessary for them to live and helped in divers manners so long as he lived.

> "By that time all their corn was planted, all their victuals [that were brought from England] was spent and they were only to rest on God's providence; many times at night not knowing where to have anything to sustain nature the next day, and so had need to pray that God would give them their daily

bread . . sometimes for two or three months together they neither had bread or any kind of corn.

* * * *

When the Pilgrims had no rain on their corn from the third week in May until the middle of July in 1624, "they set apart a solemn day of humiliation, to seek the Lord by humble and fervent prayer" for some eight hours in their great distress. Though the morning was clear and hot, without a cloud in the sky, at evening they were blessed with gentle showers in abundance until the parched ground was wet and soaked, much to the admiration of the Indians who witnessed their prayers and supplications for rain.

* * * *

"And whoso rightly considereth what manner of entrance, abiding, and proceedings we have had among these poor heathens [the Indians] since we came hither, will easily think that God hath some great work to do towards them. They were wont to be the most cruel and treacherous people in all these parts, even like lions; but to us [Pilgrims] they have been like lambs, so kind, so submissive, and trusty, as a man may truly say, many Christians are not so kind nor sincere.

* * * *

"Thus *God preserved the vine,* which *his own right hand had planted* and has enlarged our borders, by giving to us the heritage of the heathen, which they justly forfeited by their unreasonable rebellion. Oh! that the people of this, and the other colonies, would praise the Lord for his goodness, and wonderful works unto them."

Upon the death, in 1667, of Mr. John Wilson, for thirty-seven years pastor in Boston, one who signed himself J. M. wrote some blank verse from which I quote a few lines:

> "Ah! now there's none who does not know,
>   That this day in our Israel
> Is fall'n a great good man too,
>   A Prince, I might have said as well:
> A man of princely power with God,
>   For faith and love of princely spirit;
> Our Israel's chariots, horsemen good,
>   By faith and prayer, though not by merit!"

Moses in Exodus 31:13 was commanded:
"Speak thou also unto the children of Israel, saying, Verily my sabbaths ye shall keep: for it is a sign between me and you throughout your generations; that ye may know that I am the Lord that doth sanctify you."

Your Pilgrim Forefathers kept the Sabbath as did the British from whom they sprang, and the Anglo-Saxons are the nations and the only nations the world over who do keep it, by the law of the land as well as by general observance of doing no work, etc. At the Paris Exposition in 1889 every nation had their exhibit wide open on the Sabbath day as on the other six days of the week, save for two exceptions. Both the United States and Great Britain closed their sections each Saturday and did not open them until Monday morning—why I wonder?

Israel was to keep the Sabbaths throughout Israel's generations and 'twas a sign between Him and us as to who we are.

Well, here we are, the only people on earth (with our cousins, the Jews) keeping God's Sabbath! We keep the day of the risen Lord and the Jews who do not believe Christ is the risen Lord continue keeping the old Sabbath.

By that brand alone we are Israel, or I am a Dutchman and do not know how to reason from promise to performance!

Every Sabbath of the year the Protestant Episcopal Church all over the United States of America repeat from their Prayer Book the *Benedictus or Jubilate Deo*. They say they are God's chosen people, Israel, and yet some of their ministers will, I am certain, be heaving half-bricks my way, because of statements taken from the Bible to explain this. As I have lived most of my life on a diet of half-bricks, I'm certain that a few extra ones, even at the hands of my friends the parsons, won't do me much harm, and the exercise may do them some good, they often need it.

BENEDICTUS	REMARKS
St. Luke Chap. I. [68] Blessed be the Lord God of Israel; for he hath visited and redeemed his people;	Jesus said he came but to "the lost sheep of the house of Israel"— "my heritage," "my chosen," "my dispersed," "my outcasts," "my inheritance," "my first-born," "my sheep," "my witnesses," "mine elect," "the well beloved of my soul," "the Lord's flock," "my servants," "my nation," and "my people Israel," and he knew whereof he spoke,

158 THE DESTINY OF AMERICA

BENEDICTUS	REMARKS
[69] And hath raised up a mighty salvation for us; in the house of his servant David;	Jesus was of the royal seed of David and was raised up for us and has been our salvation; and through us the whole world has had an opportunity for salvation.
	The ruling house of Windsor is also descended from David's seed and so belongs to the House and Throne of David.
[70] As he spake by the mouth of his holy prophets: which have been since the world began;	Every prophecy inspired by God has or will come true at its ordained time.
[71] That we should be saved from our enemies: and from the hand of all that hate us.	As we have been. This has been made true down through the ages. November 11, 1918, was one recent example of hundreds. The hand of those who hate us has never succeeded in downing God's "battle axe" and His servants.
[72] To perform the mercy promised to our forefathers: and to remember his Holy covenant;	Have we carried out our part after being saved from our enemies? Have we remembered the Covenant God made with our forefathers? I doubt it!
[73] To perform the oath which he swore to our forefather Abraham: that he would give us;	Every item promised by any of the prophets has been fulfilled. Manasseh (U.S.A.), forgetfulness, has left undone much; they do however take on high ideals quicker than any of the other Anglo-Saxon-Celtic nations. The British flag to-day floats over all the land given to Abraham and Israel by a Covenant.
[74] That we being delivered out of the hand of our enemies: might serve him without fear;	Are you doing this freely or has mammon first call?

BENEDICTUS	REMARKS
[75] In holiness and righteousness before him: all the days of our life.	Are we doing our best along this line?
[76] And thou, child, shalt be called the prophet of the Highest: for thou shalt go before the face of the Lord to prepare his ways;	John the Baptist who preached repentance as the first step in the knowledge of salvation.
[77] To give knowledge of salvation unto *his people* for the remission of their sins.	All Anglo-Saxondom and most of the world have had this knowledge given them through his 10 servants Israel of the Anglo-Saxon breeds.
[78] Through the tender mercy of our God: whereby the day-spring [or light] from on high hath visited us [Israel];	Christ said he came but to the "lost sheep of the house of Israel." He was the light that through Israel was to lighten the whole world. And he left his Kingdom on earth in charge of his ten servants the Ten Tribes until He should come again. See Luke 19: verses 12, 13. The light has shone through Israel and over the face of the whole earth.
[79] To give light to them that sit in darkness, and in the shadow of death: and to guide our feet into the way of peace.	Goodness knows the world that sits in darkness as to the Creator's plan has much need of redemption through His executives the Anglo-Saxon nations, His servant Israel and the seed of David who are to rule until Christ comes again, this time to take the Kingdom.

If this Book of Common Prayer is also a book of common sense, it must mean what it says. Why say we will be saved from all our enemies —which was promised only to Israel—if we are not Israel? Parsons, long-haired and short are invited to answer that question the next time they repeat the Benedictus to their congregations.

Never in the world's history has there been such a need for divine guidance to guide our feet into the way of peace as in this year 1921 A.D.

When we had our back to the wall in the spring of 1918, when Germany was making her final thrust to dominate this world, materially, politically and religiously, every Anglo-Saxon nation, colony or settlement (all Israel) got on their knees in prayer and humiliation before the Supreme Ruler of this universe and admitting their sins and shortcomings, asked for divine guidance and strength to win through,—as you did in Abraham Lincoln's time.

We won through and I've often since wondered how many people really recognize who won the war. Every nation secretly thinks it was the big factor, but surely it was the God of Israel! God used our nations as His battle axe and weapons of war, and through His help we finally won the war while the politicians of your country and Britain have lost us the peace.

Read Isaiah; its all good and its so hard to pick from the many, many references one that is better than the rest! Take the 49th Chapter for instance:

> 1. "Listen, O isles, unto me [the Brith-ish or Covenant Isles]; and hearken, ye people, from far" [U.S.A., Australia, New Zealand, Canada, South Africa, etc., all "from far."]

THE DESTINY OF AMERICA 161

3. "Thou art my servant, O Israel, in whom I will be glorified.

6. "I will also give thee [Israel] for a light to the Gentiles, that thou mayest be my salvation unto the end of the earth."

Well, who have been the peoples to carry the light, God's laws and commandments and light, to the Gentiles and to the ends of the earth? God's servants, Israel, were to do it. The Anglo-Saxons alone have done it, therefore, the Anglo-Saxons are Israel. Note in Chapter VII. where the Protestant missionary societies have almost 100,000 missionaries and helpers working. Britain and her offspring are doing what Israel was to do, therefore Britain, America, Australia, Canada, Newfoundland, New Zealand, South Africa and the other Anglo-Saxon Celtic communities the world over are God's chosen people, His instruments, Israel, which means "ruling with God."* They have a divine commission and the specifications are interwoven throughout both the Old and the New Testaments, that the wise who search the Scriptures may understand. Had the Anglo-Saxons the world round made a proper job of "searching the Scriptures" as they were instructed to do, they would be wise on how to deal with all the problems that now afflict the world. What would that be worth in dollars and cents to America in this 1921st year of our Lord? How much? What would you give to know how

---
*Young's analytical concordance.

business prospects were going to pan out for the next five, ten or fifteen years?

There are hundreds of statements made about Israel in the Bible, and no nation or assortment of nations other than the Anglo-Saxon-Celtic nations can fulfill or have fulfilled the prophecies laid down, and I know of no single instance of a prophecy about Israel that the Anglo-Saxon people can not and do not fill to the very letter.

Let us take for instance this statement of the prophet Isaiah, born about 778 B.C.:

> "Thus saith the Lord, in an acceptable time have I heard thee [Israel], and in a day of salvation have I helped thee: and I will preserve thee, and give thee for a covenant of the people, to establish the earth, to cause to inherit the desolate heritages." (Isa. 49:8.)

If ever a nation was helped when they sought salvation, surely it has been our forefathers of Brith-ish or covenant stock; and Israel has been preserved and given for "a covenant of the people, to establish the earth, and to cause to inherit the desolate heritages."

I take the following facts from Whittaker's Almanac for 1920 to establish the fact that this promise to Israel has been fulfilled up to date and is still going strong.

Americans feel proud of their flag, Old Glory, and they do well! But what about their "Older Glory," the flag that braved a thousand years the battle and the breeze, the glorious Union Jack? To-day it proudly floats over the following countries, in Europe, Asia, Africa, Australia, and Canada, as a visible evidence that the British (Ephraim) section of Israel is carrying out her God-given covenant to establish the earth, however imperfectly,—still no other nation is doing it so well, and we may well remember that there is nothing perfect under the sun and even it is alleged to have spots on it!

Waste places settled by Ephraim Israel

	When Acquired	How Acquired	Population
IN EUROPE			
The United Kingdom	....	....	45,500,000
Isle of Man	....	....	50,000
Channel Islands	1066	Duke Normandy....	97,000
Malta and Gozo	1814	Treaty Cession	211,000
Gibraltar	1713	Treaty Cession	20,000
IN ASIA.			
Indian Empire	1757-1897	Conquest	315,000,000
Ceylon	1802	Treaty Cession	4,000,000
Straits Settlements	1785-1909	Treaty Cession	700,000
Fed. Malay States.	1874-1888	Treaty Cession	1,000,000
Other Malay States.	1842-1900	Treaty Cession	800,000
Hong Kong	1842-1906	Treaty Cession	440,000
Weihaiwei	1898	Treaty Cession	130,000
North Borneo	1877	Cession	204,000
Brunei	1888	Treaty Cession	30,000
Sarawak	1888	Proctectorate	650,000
Cyprus	1914	Annexation	275,000
IN AFRICA.			
Cape Province	1814	Treaty Cession	....
Natal	1843	Annexation	....
Transvaal	1900	Annexation	....
Orange Free State..	1900	Annexation	5,000,000
South West Province	1914	Conquest	120,000
Basutoland	....	Conquest	350,000
Bechuanaland	1895	Conquest	126,000

164 THE DESTINY OF AMERICA

	When Acquired	How Acquired	Population
Rhodesia	1889	Conquest	1,700,000
Gambia	1807	Treaty Cession	146,000
Gold Coast	1787	Treaty Cession	1,400,000
Sierra Leone	1787	Treaty Cession	1,100,000
Northern Nigeria	1891	Treaty Cession	10,000,000
Southern Nigeria	1891	Treaty Cession	7,000,000
German West Africa	1914	Conquest & Mandate	4,000,000
Somaliland	1884	Treaty Cession	300,000
East Africa	1888-1918	Conquest & Cession	10,000,000
Uganda	1894	Treaty Cession	2,500,000
Zanzibar	1890	Treaty Cession	200,000
Nyassaland	1891	Treaty Cession	1,000,000
Egypt	1882	Occupation	12,000,000
Soudan	1898	Conquest	2,000,000
Mauritius	1810-1814	Conquest & Cession.	370,000
Seychelles	1814	Treaty Cession	23,000
Ascension	1815	Occupation	150
St. Helena	1675	Conquest	3,500

IN AUSTRALIA.

New South Wales	1788	Settlement	650,000
Victoria	1832	Settlement	320,000
South Australia	1826	Settlement	409,000
Queensland	1824	Settlement	606,000
Tasmania	1803	Settlement	191,000
West Australia	1828	Settlement	282,000
New Zealand	1835	Settlement and Conquest	1,050,000
Fiji	1874	Cession from Natives	170,000
Papua	1884	Annexation from Natives	360,000
Pacific Islands	1895-1914	Annexation	200,000

IN AMERICA.

Newfoundland	1583	Treaty Cession	4,000,000
Jamaica	1655	Conquest	3,200,000
Bahamas	1629	Settlement	475,000
Leeward Islands	1621-1650	Settlement	676,000
Windward Islands	1763-1783	Cession	800,000
Barbadoes	1605	Settlement	1,850,000
Trinidad & Tabogo	1797	Conquest	4,500,000
British Guiana	1803-1814	Conquest & Cession.	2,500,000
British Honduras	1798	Conquest & Cession.	500,000
Bermuda	1612	Settlement	736,000
Falkland Islands	1771	Treaty Cession	600,000
South Georgia	1771		

	When Acquired	How Acquired	Population
Ontario	1759-1762	Conquest & Cession)	
Quebec	1759-1762	Conquest & Cession)	
Nova Scotia	1657-1713	Conquest & Cession)	
New Brunswick	1763	Treaty & Cession..)	
Prince Edward Isl..	1745	Conquest ....)	
British Columbia	1670	Settlement ....)	
Manitoba	1813	Settlement ....)	
Alberta	1670	Settlement ....)	
Saskatchewan	1670	Settlement ....)	
North West Terr'tes	1670	Settlement ....)	7,200,000

Quite a list for the Mother of Free Parliaments to take on in a few hundred years since she began to settle the waste places of the earth!

What glorious comment on Brith-ish or Covenant rule was presented to the world when His Majesty Our King and Governor in 1915 sent out a call for more men! By hundreds of thousands, aye by millions they, like the disciples of old, dropped everything and followed the call to save the world from the forces of evil bent on destroying with fire and sword that human freedom which the Anglo-Saxon civilization had through centuries been the means of preserving and building up.

Behind our front lines where civilized methods of burial could prevail, every British soldier, from Tommy to the topmost general who lost his life in the cause, wrapped in his army blanket was taken to the cemetery under the folds of that grand old banner, the British Ensign, for Christian burial; and to-day their bodies lie in thousands, row on row, while they rest in God in peace, and their rest shall be glorious.

IN FLANDERS' FIELDS.

(Written by Col. John McCrea of Guelph,
Ontario, Canada, Serving in
France, 1917.)

In Flanders' fields the poppies blow
    Between the crosses, row on row,
That mark our place, and in the sky
    The larks still bravely singing fly,
Scarce heard amid the guns below.
    We are the dead. Short days ago
We lived, felt dawn, saw sunset glow,
    Loved and were loved, and now we lie
        In Flanders' fields.

Take up the quarrel with the foe
    To you, from falling hands we throw
The Torch—be yours to hold it high.
    If ye break faith with us who die
We shall not sleep though poppies grow
        In Flanders' fields.

AMERICA'S ANSWER.

(Written by R. W. Lillard and appeared
in the New York *Evening Post*.)

Rest ye in peace, ye Flanders' dead,
    The fight that ye so bravely lead
We've taken up. And we will keep
    True faith with you who lie asleep
With each a cross to mark his bed
    And poppies blowing overhead
Where once his own life blood ran red
        In Flanders' fields.

Fear not that ye have died for naught
    The Torch ye threw to us is caught
Ten million hands will hold it high;
    And freedom's light shall never die.
We've learned the lesson that ye taught
        In Flanders' fields.

Thus did the souls of millions from the land of Brother Jonathan respond to the appeal of the little poem "In Flanders' Fields," whose author later gave his life in the cause.

Did you ever read Isaiah 11:12 and wonder whether that ensign was the British ensign? The King of Great Britain and Ireland and of the Brith-ish Dominions beyond the seas, Emperor of India, is clearly of the seed of David as is proved in *Britain an Enduring Dynasty* by Milner, and the ensign which that root of Jesse floats is the Union Jack. To it the Gentiles do seek in Palestine and do rest under its folds. Britain first and later America have been a haven of rest for the oppressed of all the Gentile nations. "And his rest shall be glorious." Peace in Britain has been proverbial for centuries. 'Tis a bit unsettled at present, but even at that, Britain is more settled than any other nation, with the possible exception of the United States of America.

Isaiah 11: 12.

Authorized Version	*Ferrar Fenton's Translation.*
And he shall set up an ensign for the nations, and shall assemble the outcasts of Israel, and gather together the dispersed of Judah from the four corners of the earth.	And then He will raise up a Flag to the Heathen, And all Israel's wanderers, and Judah's Dispersion From the four Wings of the earth will collect.

What would we say are the facts in connection with this prophecy? I figure it out in this way: Firstly, the British when they took possession of the Holy Land and City hoisted their ensign; and under the freedom of its folds all classes of heathen and nationalities are collecting for protection, and for rest from the persecutions under the Turkish, Russian and other flags. Secondly, the Jews are, representatively, hiking back to the Holy Land from the four corners of the earth and under a Governor from Israel, Sir Herbert Samuels; and they will continue to come until the Holy Land will again blossom as the rose, as was predicted three thousand years ago.

It may not be amiss to point out that the first national flag of the United States was called "The Grand Union" and carried the Union Jack in the upper corner as does the Canadian, Australian, New Zealand and other Anglo-Saxon nations. This flag was composed of thirteen stripes of alternate white and red, one for each British colony, and in the upper corner was the British Union Jack of that period displaying the two crosses of St. George and St. Andrews, as introduced in 1707.

"This American Grand Union flag was raised by Washington over the camp of his Army at Cambridge, Mass., on January 1st, 1776, to the accompanying salute of thirteen guns.

"By this flag the 13 colonies testified that though in arms, they still claimed to be Britons and were demanding for themselves all the rights of citizenship which such relation conferred."

The first American flag called the "Grand Union", hoisted by Washington over his camp.
(The colors being red, white and blue).

(See page 168)

ISRAEL HEIR OF THE WORLD

(See page 232)

THE DESTINY OF AMERICA

"On July 4th, 1776, The Declaration of Independence followed but this Grand Union flag still continued to be used as the National flag by the 13 States and it was not until about a year later, June 14th, 1777, that a new national flag was fully developed.*

American Section of waste places promised to Israel

	Date	How Secured	Population
Alaska	1867	Purchased	100,000
Philippine Islands	1898	Capture	7,635,000
Guam	1898		15,000
Hawaii Islands	1897		250,000
Porto Rico	1899		1,120,000
Tutuila	1898		7,250
Wake and Johnson Isls.	1899		
Aleutian Islands	1867		2,000
Virgin Islands	1917		27,000
Panama	1904		

The United States have been so busy establishing the immense continent the Almighty selected for them that your outside possessions are not yet very extensive. "I will preserve thee [Israel]"—what for? "To establish the earth, to cause to inherit the desolate heritages." You are *Manasseh*-Israel, and your job is to carry out this commission, helping to establish these places. It is quite as much your job as it is John Bull's. Some day you will have to give an account of what you did with "the talents" committed to your care. 'Twill be of little use to plead: our politicians did it. Who elected them? Who is responsible for them? America's

---

*History of the Union Jack by Barlow Cumberland.

business men, individually; and the nation, nationally. America will have to buck the line instead of crawling under the barn when asked to take a few shares of Israel's burden in desolate places like Armenia. America's commission was not to live to itself alone. Read Matthew 25 and note verses 31 and 32 particularly:

> "When the Son of man shall come in his glory . . . . . Before him shall be gathered all nations: and he shall separate them one from another, as a shepherd divideth his sheep from the goats."

America's national stand during the next fifteen years will be decisive in more ways than one. It's up to you, gentlemen! You have had the wealth of the mine, the forest, the sea and the fertile earth all at your command and you will have to give an account of your stewardship; because God has given you His plan to work to, which covers all the details you would require during your lifetime, even if you lived to be a hundred, and shows how you were to invest and how you were to spend the talents—golden ones—He put in your way.

The "kingdom" spoken of in verse 34 will be right here on earth. In that day how many of your citizens and ours will wish they had spent their time, their energies and their magnificient organizing ability, as did that prince in America's section of Israel, Herbert Hoover, clothing the naked and feeding the poor?—while your and our profiteers were profiting on the most urgent needs of humanity (and this includes Labor Unions' wage profiteers) during the war. Hoover and the type he represents were all giving their time for world service, which is our job, because Israel was to break and has broken the back of every menace to liberty that has threatened the world for hundreds of years and Hoover and others in more humble positions will get the rewards for such princely service "to the least of these."

Say, reader, if you want to get in on a good thing, in on the ground floor of a good thing, a better one than any stockbroker you know can put you next to, just read the Bible through; and every time you see Israel mentioned in its dispatches, just say, "That's we-uns" or "us-all" and just note the job or work given to Israel, both the Manasseh (U.S.A.) and Ephraim (English) sections, and particularly note what is due for the next fifteen years to Britain and to America, as you are going to be in it up to the neck.

Harvey O. Higgins asks in March *McClures* "Is there something wrong with the American Mind?" There most certainly is, Harvey! but your dissecting knife did not remove it. The Soul of America knows more than the reasoning mind of America can either see or understand. America's Soul was in seething unrest while for two years you were cautioned to be neutral in thought, word and deed. How free you felt the day your first citizen declared America at war with Germany! The fetters binding America's Soul burst their bonds and freed the liberty-loving spirit they had in thrall. We at the Front, three to four thousand miles away, in spirit saw your shackles broken off and were glad, but no more happy than were the millions of Americans who had scarcely been able to look your brother Canadians, Britons, and Frenchmen in the eye because they were saving the world for America as much as they were for Canada, Britain or France and they and you knew it.

To-day America's Soul is again filled with unrest, and Dr. O'Higgins prods the patient in the back, in the front, in this corner and in that and asks is the pain here or there, and finally with a flourish he shouts: "I have it! It's the effect of your Pilgrim Forefathers' 'repression and Soul fear' that still sticks in the fifty-five per cent. of Americans descended from the Puritans!" I wonder if he is right? Not being a doctor or even a chiropractor, one hesitates to say; but being a Roadbuilder, one is not afraid to hazard a guess that the Soul of America knows more than its politicians understand. If Dr. O'Higgins is correct, he has only touched the fringe of the cause, because back of your Pilgrim

THE DESTINY OF AMERICA 173

Puritan forefathers are your Brith-ish forefathers, and back of them are your Israel forefathers until you go back back to Joseph, Jacob, Isaac and Abraham, who was God's friend, a friend willing to go wherever God directed.

The Soul of America, in my opinion, is troubled, because since the Armistice, your ideals (and no nation has had higher ones) have been temporarily scrapped and you apparently have had no Washington, no Lincoln, no Roosevelt to point the way in clear unmistakable tones and lead the nation towards its real goal.

France was the friend of America at the time of America's greatest need! America stood silent for years, while France bled at every pore in saving the world from destruction, before General John Pershing stood in France beside the monument of that noble Frenchman who fought for America and saluting it said, "Lafayette, we are here!"

France spent almost everything she had; one and a half millions of her citizen soldiers lie buried along her battle-front from Ostend to Switzerland. Her maimed and wounded by the ten thousands still fill her hospitals.

To-day Germany is winning the peace by the same bare-faced trickery her Von Bernstorfs and Von Papens practiced in the United States during the war, and what is America doing to help her friend of yesterday, France?

France owes America some dollars for shells used to protect your homes as well as hers.

America owes France the lives of the million and a half of her citizen soldiers, which France spent to make safe the world. America proposes to collect her dollars. WILL SHE REPAY FRANCE HER LIVES SPENT IN THIS WORLD CAUSE?

If the Soul of America was not restless and unsettled under such a condition 'twere almost useless to have souls.

If America and Britain knew what the law laid down by God in his National Constitution, laws and statutes for all Israel nations was, they would not hesitate for a day as to the proper and only actions to take in this matter of debt. Every Israelitish debtor had to be released every seven years and the debt charged up to God who gives his word that He will repay it!

Is His credit good in America? Does "in God we trust" on your national coins to-day mean what it says? If it does, you are challenged by God's constitution for America to forego all interest, and at the end of seven years the principle, and He will repay it.

God promises such an outpouring of His spirit when Israel sees and believes God's plan for world redemption that they will become a nation of priests, when no longer will it be necessary for a preacher to say, "Know the Lord,"

THE DESTINY OF AMERICA

because all shall know Him, from the least to the greatest.

America's Soul knows that this is in the offing and will be unsettled and restless until she is doing her share to make God's Kingdom on earth known to all the world and especially in the home acres where the Bible containing God's instructions and prophecies is a much unread book to the old families raised here for generations as well as to the many who have swarmed into the country.

America's eyes as well as Britain's eyes are to be opened, so it's up to you to personally rustle and get on to your job and study the plans laid down by Almighty God, from whom Abraham Lincoln and George Washington sought help and from whom they received the wisdom and judgment they possessed, and they humbly walked with God, thus seeking His aid and receiving it in due measure.

CHAPTER IX.

1. American politicians twisting the old Lion's tail and kicking it in the ribs.
2. Nations surprised when British and American Fleets cooperate at Alexandria in 1882.
3. Why we could not lose South Africa despite Kaiser William's congratulations to Paul Kruger.
4. "Listen, O isles (British) unto Me and harken ye people from afar" [Americans et al."]
5. What the ships of Tarshish (Britain) have to do with their sons from afar.
6. Where was and where is Tarshish?
7. Why the daughters of Tarshish had to settle in Britain.
8. Britons in Homer's time—850 years B.C.—were the leading manufacturers in bright iron, gold, silver and lead, and her merchants furnished it for Solomon's Temple.
9. Apes and peacocks were exported then just as pigs (iron and steel) are now and they were just as little real apes and peacocks as iron and steel are real pigs now.
10. Herodotus, Pliny, Diodorus, Strabo, Homer, Ezekiel, Sir Edward Cressey and many others shew that Britain is the Isles of the West or Tarshish.

11. America's place is alongside of Britain, Canada, Australia, South Africa, *et al,* in the War of Armageddon.
12. The Kaiser's sister wondered what they would do with "Poor Wilhelm".
13. Armageddon plainly set out in the Bible. We are heading for it now.

CHAPTER IX

In 1879 Rev. Joseph Wild, then preaching in Brooklyn, N.Y., published a book, *The Lost Ten Tribes of Israel,* in which he predicted the breakup of Russia within fifty years, the taking of Jerusalem and Palestine from Turkey and the giving of it to the Jews for a national home.

This student of Israel about that time had also predicted that the United States of America would help Britain in her next war with Egypt; though at the time most U.S.A. politicians were so busy twisting the old lion's tail and kicking it in the ribs, almost without provocation save to secure the Irish vote, that anyone who predicted that they would work together was considered more kinds of a fool than is permissible to put in print.

When 1882 came around and the world saw with surprise and some nations with deep resentment, that an American fleet did help the British fleet at Alexandria, Egypt, my Scotch instinct and reason told me that the Reverend Doctor's dope along prophetic lines was good stuff and proved to me the value of the Bible prophecies.

THE DESTINY OF AMERICA

A certain merry-eyed, dimpled-cheeked young lady attended the Reverend Dr. Wild's church each evening, and I soon found my unattached feet straying thitherward not, I am afraid, for the sole purpose of absorbing spiritual truths, but for the pleasure of walking home with the aforementioned dimples in the twilight.

However, I did absorb Bible facts that have never left me; though I am afraid I have not always made the best use of them, as I am just an ordinary everyday sinner like yourself, without as yet, my wife says, any sign of sprouting wings—and believe me, she knows!

When the South African war was at its height, I was much disturbed at the outlook after the Boers "did in" General Buller's army and his reports came trickling through time after time: "I regret to report." I remember asking Dr. Wild if Britain was going to lose South Africa. "No Sir! She will win. Great Britain is only to lose one of her offspring, according to the Bible, and she lost that a hundred years and more ago when Manasseh (U.S.A.) section set up in national business for themselves as had been foretold. Its not on the cards," he said, "that Great Britain will lose another Colony." And she didn't, though at that time not a nation the world round seemed to be her friend, and the Kaiser, with almost satanic glee, cabled his congratulations to that great Boer leader, Paul Kruger, on his success.

Here are some messages the Prophet Isaiah addressed to the Brith Colony in Brith-ain, which colony had been there many, many hundreds of years when he sent this epistle to them about 712 B.C., and they would be as well known in the Home acres as is Alaska known to Washington to-day, because of the unending commerce between them.

> 49:1. "Listen, O isles [the British or Covenant Isles], unto me; and hearken, ye people, from far [the Americans, Canadians, Australians, New Zealanders, South Africans, etc.].
> 3. "Thou art my servant, O Israel, in whom I will be glorified. [In the Anglo-Saxon nations, God's name has been glorified down through the centuries.]
> 8. "Thus saith the Lord, In an acceptable time have I heard thee, and in a day of salvation have I helped thee: and I will preserve thee, and give thee for a covenant of the people, to establish the earth, to cause to inherit the desolate heritages;

The Anglo-Saxon Celts have inherited the earth—the last war pitched a hundred and fifty million heathen into Mother Britain's lap and made her responsible for their up-bringing. What a white man's burden!

> 9. "That thou mayest say to the prisoners, Go forth; to them that are in darkness, Shew yourselves. They shall feed in the ways, and their pastures shall be in all high places.
> 12. "Behold, these shall come from far: and, lo, these from the north and from the west; and these

from the land of Sinim [South—The Vulgate has it Australi].

59:18. "According to their deeds, accordingly he will repay, fury to his adversaries, recompense to his enemies; *to the islands* he will repay recompense." [Brith-ain of the Islands has been recompensed for her work among the lesser breeds without the Law].

60:9. "Surely the isles shall wait for me, and the ships of Tarshish first, to bring thy sons from far, their silver and their gold with them, unto the name of the Lord thy God, and to the Holy One of Israel, because he hath glorified thee.

12. "For the nation and kingdom that will not serve thee [Israel] shall perish; yea, those nations shall be utterly wasted."

The "isles" referred to are the British Isles from which sailed the ships of Tarshish as is shown by Rev. Dr. Wm. H. Poole in his book *Anglo-Israel*, published in 1882, now out of print, from which I quote the following data on Tarshish:

"*Tarshish* was a name given to one of Noah's grandchildren. Gen. 10:4. 'And the sons of Javan, Elishah, and Tarshish, Kittim, and Dodanim.' It was the custom in those early days to name the country after the person who was the owner or ruler or chief. 'By these (persons named) were the Islands of the Gentiles divided in their lands.' To Tarshish was given the west coast of Europe and that country was so named as may be seen upon ancient maps, several of which I have before me. Upon one of these very ancient maps England is called Javan.

"The Rev. James McIntosh, curate, says '*Tarshish* when resolved into its elements is—'*tar*' a border of fringe round about and '*shish*' bright, shiny, white and means the land is white or bright round about which is the name given to England from the whiteness of its cliffs on the southern coast. No name more fitly describes England to those early traders coming northward to Britain from the Bay of Biscay.'

"In 2 Chron, 9:21: "For the king's [Solomon's] ships went to Tarshish with the servants of Huram: every three years once come the ships of Tarshish bringing gold, and silver, ivory, and apes, and peacocks.

"In Ezek. 27:12, 19: "Tarshish was thy merchant by reason of the multitude of all kind of riches; with silver, iron, tin, and lead, they traded in thy fairs.

"'Dan also and Javan going to and fro occupied in thy fairs: bright iron, cassia and calamus, were in thy market.'

"And in I Kings 10:22: 'For the king had at sea a navy of Tharshish with the navy of Hiram: once in three years came the navy of Tharshish, bringing gold, and silver, ivory, and apes, and peacocks.'"

Tyre was the great trading emporium in those days, and the bright iron, tin, and lead from Cornwall were apparently the heaviest cargo brought by the "navy of Tharshish" and Solomon's ships, both of which were used in the commerce carried on between Tyre and Tarshish.

In the 66th Chapter of Isaiah, Tarshish is mentioned in a manner confirming the above view.

Verse 19. "And I will set a sign among them, and I will send those that escape of them unto the nations, to Tarshish, Pul, and Lud, that draw the bow, to Tubal, and Javan, to the isles afar off, that have not heard my fame, neither have seen my glory; and *they shall declare my glory among the Gentiles.*"

THE DESTINY OF AMERICA

These passages make it clear that Tarshish was a long way from Palestine and was reached by sea route north and west and that Tarshish and the isles afar off were in the same direction and that Tarshish then, as now, was given to trade.

"Isaiah also affirms that the citizens of Tarshish did not worship Jehovah at that time that 'They had not heard my fame, neither seen my glory: *and also that they would, in future, become missionaries to declare my glory among the Gentiles.*' The remnant of Israel were sent to Tarshish and to the Isles of Tarshish to the Isles afar off. The "escaped" of Israel and the "preserved" of Israel were sent over to Tarshish and the Lord promised them four things—the comely, the beautiful, the excellent and the glorious."

Have not the promises been fulfilled and have not the Isles been world missionaries and the means of declaring God's glory among the Gentiles? The only answer is yes! yes!

"When the power of the Medo-Persian Empire was broken and all hindrances removed, the commission from the Lord was given to Israel, Isa. 23:6, 10: 'Pass ye over to Tarshish .... Pass through thy land as a river, O daughter of Tarshish.'

"They could now go as a river, in streams (our historians say in waves), none to hinder them, so they are commanded to go to Tarshish. They went in a series of invasions. Benjamin the last tribe going over in 1066 making the Union of Jacob complete in the Covenant land Brith-ain.

"In Psalms 72:10: 'The kings of Tarshish and of the isles shall bring presents that people on the isles of the west were a noble and generous people and they still run true to form as every calamity the world round attests in this day and generation."

"Sir Edward Cressey, a distinguished Antiquarian in his history of England says: 'The British tin mines mainly supplied the glorious adornment of Solomon's temple.'

" 'Tarshish', says Hillier, 'was the west coast of Europe, afterwards called Gaul and in later times Spain and France."

"In Ezekiel 27:12 and 15 the place and destiny of the ships is described by its merchandise and its pursuits, and again Tarshish is spoken of in connection with the trade of a western country. Of Tyre is said 'Javan was thy merchants in all riches, with silver, iron, tin and lead, they traded in thy fair and Dan (Ireland) is here associated with Javan or England." In the same chapter it is said, verse 25: 'The ships of Tarshish did sing of thee in thy market and thou wast replenished and made very glorious in the midst of the seas.'

"There is beauty and propriety in this allusion by the prophet to the sons of the Hebrew sailors as they made the name of Tyre honored, and glorious, away beyond the pillars of Hercules (Gibraltar) or as viewed from Mount Zion it would seem to be in the midst of the seas.

"All historians knew that the Western Isles supplied the East with all manner of elaborately wrought metals, of gold and silver, and brass, bright iron and tin.

THE DESTINY OF AMERICA

"In Homer, Book 18, a free translation describes the smelting operations going on in the foundries on the Tarshish Isles: Homer lived about 850 B.C."

'In hissing flames huge silver bars were rolled
  Stubborn brass and tin and solid gold.
A darker metal intrenched the place
  And piles of glittering tin the enclosure grace.'

Homer also describes the soldiers' coat of arms:

'Ten rows of azure still the work enfold
Twice ten of tin and twelve of ductile gold.'

Again:

'The shields completed vast and strong
A breastplate dazzling bright as flames of fire forged
And next a weighty helmet for his head,
  Fair, richly wrought, with crests of gold:
Then last, well fitted greaves of pliant tin.
  Now at his will, and as the work required,
The stubborn brass, and tin, and precious gold
  And silver first he melted in the fire.'

Brith-ain, at this early date, 850 B.C., was *the manufacturing centre of the world,* yet your histories and ours would have it that in Caesar's time we were skin-clad barbarians. Such lying statements are easily refuted by any student who takes the trouble to look into the facts as presented in *St. Paul in Britain* and histories that gave facts instead of fiction about our ancestors.*

---

*St. Paul in Britain, by Rev. R. W. Morgan.

Britons and Bretons have always been the advance-guard of their time in education, mode of living, methods of doing trade as well as in all forms of culture.

> "The Prophet Jeremiah 9:10, might well say 'Silver spread into plates was brought from these islands.'"

What about ivory, apes and peacocks? Did Britain export them? Sure she did in the same way iron merchants now export their iron as "pigs" by the ton. Dr. Poole says:

> "If I could peep into the ledgers of the merchants of Tarshish who spread gold and silver and brass and tin into plates for the Eastern markets, I would find in their bills of sale so many tons of Apes and Peacocks and Lambs. They used these terms as we now use "Pigs" in the iron trade. When these metals are in process of smelting and refining they give a fine specimen of the variegated hues of the Peacock's plumage and in certain processes of preparation they were named after the bird whose plumage they so much resembled. Three thousand years hence people may wonder that in our day gold eagles were so plentiful and of such high repute among us." [Since the war "there ain't no such bird" seen in commerce or exchange!]

> "Aristotle (384-322 B.C.) wrote: 'Beyond the pillars of Hercules (Gibraltar) the ocean flows around the earth. In this ocean, however, there are Islands, and those are very large and are called Britannic, Albion and Ierne, which are larger than those before named. They lie beyond the Baltic and there are not

a few small islands around the Britannic Isles and around Iberia.'

"Herodotus 484-425 B.C. describing the tin Islands in the West of Europe says: 'The tin came from Cornwall, which, when mixed with copper, formed the well-known Bronze of the early times.'

"Diodorus says: 'Tin and bright iron were brought into Gaul from the Western Isles 620 years before Christ.'

"Pliny says: 'The whole of the Roman Empire was supplied with metals and tin from Britannia. He says Greece too was supplied with tin and sundry metals from the same source 907 B.C.'

"Strabo, born 63 B.C., informs us of a Phoenician captain who destroyed a rival ship rather than let the crew know where Tarshish was or how to land their vessels at Tarshish.

"To Javan was given the Brith (or covenant) Isles. Those Isles on the ancient maps and in the Bible are called Isles of the West and Isles of Tarshish. To Javan's two sons, Tarshish and Kittim, was given the Western Coast of Europe, Spain, Portugal, and France.

"Xenophon, who wrote 100 years later than Ezekiel, described one of those ships of Tarshish starting for *Gades*, which is Latin for Cadiz, on the Atlantic coast of Spain."

These and dozens of other references show that Spain, Portugal and France were called Tarshish and that the Isles of Tarshish were the adjoining British Islands. Having gotten that key in your right hand you are now in a position to unlock doors that have puzzled Bible students without it, for ages. Now take, for instance, Armageddon, that great war which America and the world has still to fight.

I was much interested recently listening to that great war correspondent and student of past and current events in Europe, Sir Philip Gibbs, a typical Englishman, quiet, thoughtful, self-effacing, delivering a lecture "without a superlative, almost without emphasis, and without flambuoyancy"—the kind that we all so much enjoy, and some of us wish we could imitate; but we regretfully realize that, like British lawns, it takes time and education to grow that sort.

Well, Sir Philip said there were still two chances for war within ten years, one was by a union of Russia and Germany, and the other by an alliance between Russia and the Mohammedans. For the information of Sir Philip Gibbs and any others who may desire same, it may be mentioned that the Bible says that Russia will take advantage of both these unions. Russia is to combine with Prussia and also with all the Mohammedan and pagan nations, and led by "the Chief Prince of Rosh" will make their final world drive for the Holy Land, Constantinople and the Suez Canal. It is estimated that it will be timed to commence

THE DESTINY OF AMERICA

about 1928 and end about 1936, and according to prophecy this will be the last war on this war-cursed earth for 1,000 years. I wrote to that effect last year to one of Britain's ablest army commanders, but he could not agree, saying Armageddon could not come for fifty years,—not a great war. Another British Army commander wrote that it could not come before a hundred years or Europe would be bankrupt; but either they or the stone Bible, the Pyramid, is mistaken and I'm sure they will both approve of my backing my faith on the latter, as up to date its predictions have come true for the outstanding events in Israel's history since the world began.

The Pyramid of Gizeh is the oldest building in the world. It is without question the most wonderful building in the world to-day, though built by Shem, son of Noah, 2170 B.C. It was built, I believe, under divine guidance, because it foretells in stone and in Hebrew measurements what the Bible foretells in Hebrew words—the outstanding prophecies made concerning God's chosen Hebrew people, both the House of Judah and the House of Israel and even located their being joined together in Jerusalem before Armageddon. Isaiah said (Isa. 19:19, 20): "In that day shall there be an altar to the Lord in the midst of the land of Egypt, and a pillar at the border thereof to the Lord. And it shall be for a sign and for a witness unto the Lord of hosts in the land of Egypt." Well, Mr. Business Man, there she stands just where they said it would be, over four thousand years old, God's witness giving visible, tangible confirmation to the prophecies contained in our Bible. And yet, men sometimes wonder if there is an unseen Ruler of the universe! To-day you can rub your hands over the measurements in enduring granite showing when the far-seeing and divinely inspired architect indicated that Armageddon would start and finish and as yet you and your leaders are blind to this visible evidence placed in Egypt, your early home, for your and your nation's guidance.

Why? And again why?

Is it because the learned professors in your universities mostly "finished" their education in Germany and absorbed so much of that German-Jewish-made antichristian higher criticism that belittles and pooh-poohs the "more sure word of prophecy" and makes light of the bulk of our Bible that they fail to see God's prophecies being made good by history every year that we are on His earth.

Mr. D. Davidson, M.C., M.C.I, one of the wisest students of the recent developments in Pyramid Chronology points out in the September issue of the *Covenant People* how the Pyramid in measurements in stone showed war was overhanging Israel from November 8, 1912, the time of the Balkan troubles, and how from August

THE DESTINY OF AMERICA

4th, 1914, Israel had to bend her back and was not free to stand upright until we passed through the low passage which extended in these stone measurements from August 4th, 1914, to November 11th, 1918, when again Israel peoples could stand erect and breathe freely with war removed by the Armistice.

July 12th, 1920, Israel again had to bow her head and pass under two removable yokes which extend until November 10th, 1921. These may be the yokes that Labor and the Sinn Fein Irish have placed upon all Israel, but whatever they are they will be removed November 10th, 1921, when again we can stand upright until 1928 ushers in the time of trouble foretold as that great day of God Almighty, Armageddon.

Our allies in Armageddon will be Sheba, which is India, Dedan, which is Arabia (the sons of Ishmael, who were always to dwell in tents as they always have, and who were to become a nation, as they did when that young Englishman, Colonel Lawrence, formed them into one during the late war; and Winston Churchill has now made an Arab ally, Feisul, King of Mesopotamia;) the "merchants of Tarshish" (recently termed the "Shopkeepers of Britain"); and all the young lions thereof.

The shopkeepers of Britain (formerly the "merchants of Tarshish") and their contemptible little army were referred to by his nibs, the alleged all highest Emperor Wilhelm of Germany, now doing time at Doorn, and dodging tax paying. In 1887 Queen Victoria of Great Britain and Ireland was presented with a chart showing her descent from King Divid of Jerusalem, and a copy was also sent to the Emperor of Germany. Bill of the upturned moustache secured this data, believed it and thought, being the eldest son of Queen Victoria's eldest daughter, that he was the King Pin in Israel, and so was God's battle-axe and weapons of war, which he figured were made for Germany, hence all his blather about "Me und Gott," etc., and his condescension in taking *Gott* into *partnership* with him in his war schemes and placing "*Gott mit uns*" on the belt of every soldier who wore a German uniform. Had he been as wise as he was vain, he would have remembered that "by their fruits ye shall know them" applies to all nations, peoples and churches, kings and rulers. All are not Israel who say they are, but many are of the congregation of Satan! The Kaiser and his nation will yet receive the punishment due for their outrages against humanity, against Israel and against God the creator and ruler of this universe. They cannot possibly dodge it.

When in Germany, a friend asked if I would like to meet the Kaiser's eldest sister, as we were temporarily living under the same roof, her palace being occupied as Headquarters of the Corps Canadian.

THE DESTINY OF AMERICA

"Sure, I'd like to do anything once, provided it did not cost too much," I said. So we were introduced and spent a pleasant hour deciphering autographs in an album and reading character from them, though we were not supposed to fraternize at that time. But seeing a British staff general present when we entered, my conscience did not trouble me; besides, rules and regulations were never a Canadian's long suit in the army or elsewhere.

Well, the Princess was quite concerned in those days about "poor Wilhelm"! and wondered to me, mind you, what they would do with him! Now, I had a whole lot of things I'd wanted to do to him for four and a half years but the situation forbade me mentioning them in detail, to his relative. Perhaps it was my temporary military training that prevented me from making a direct reply to the Princess' pointed question. Anyway, I sidestepped it and turned the conversation on to a side line. What wouldn't I give to be able to "spill all the beans" I gathered in that chateau! 'Twould make interesting reading but 'tisn't done, even among Canadians.

Well, who else do you suppose are going to take part with the "merchants of Tarshish" in the great battle of Armageddon? The Kaiser referred to the British as a nation of "shopkeepers," and we often speak of the old British Lion. Well, at Armageddon, there will be "the merchants of Tarshish'' and beside them will be "all the young lions thereof."

> "Sheba, and Dedan, and the merchants of Tarshish, with all the young lions thereof, shall say unto thee, Art thou come to take a spoil? Hast thou gathered thy company to take a prey? To carry away silver and gold, To take away cattle and goods, To take a great spoil?.... In that day when my people of Israel dwelleth safely, shalt thou [Chief Prince of Rosh *et al*] not know it? And thou shalt come up against my people of Israel, as a cloud to cover the land; it shall be in the latter days." (Ezek. 38:13, 14, 16).

This war is to take place in the Holy Land and will be finished by 1936 according to the best authorities and as I have shown that America is a young lion from Britain, or the Covenant Land, the first born and the strongest of the old lion's cubs, and as the Bible specifically says that *all* the young lions will be there, America must be and will be on the job as she was at Alexandria in 1882. A fine healthy lot of use there will be in this land war for capital dreadnaught ships at forty million dollars a throw! Fast cruisers and destroyers, yes, and ships for carrying troops, and aeroplanes, etc., yes, though I see your air officers' estimates for such aeroplane ships have been canned and chucked into the waste basket by Congress. "Who is blind but my servant Israel?"

What will it cost America when she enters Armageddon unprepared I wonder? If Americans knew their prospects and future they would fear Japan as little as they now fear Canada, Australia or New Zealand.

Armageddon and the forces who will fight it are plainly shaping up to-day for this war as were the forces of Germany getting ready, and discernibly so by students of warfare like Lord Roberts, Admiral Sir John Fisher, and our Late King Edward for fourteen years before 1914, and yet, instead of preparing for it, your vote-catching politicians, your Hearsts, your Sinn Feiners and pro-Germans are all trying to stir up strife between Brother John of the Isles and Brother Jonathan from afar who will each need the help of Japan and of each other as never before in their histories.

I wish I had the time to elaborate upon what the Bible tells of this coming war and lay down the plan of campaign for it, but its beyond my limit of time and I have already strung this much farther than I had intended, until, I fear I will be wearing out my welcome staying so long at my first visit and partaking of such a hearty meal while marking out for you this bridgehead.

That reminds me of a hotel I used to patronize in my younger days where they gave you a good full farmer's dinner, chicken or roast beef for twenty-five cents per head, which sounds almost unreal now. Well, this proprietor was a real "Boniface" with a sign above his sideboard which read:

"Eat Hearty and give the House a Good Name."

I wish I could with confidence hang out such a sign for you to eat heartily of the food contained in this screed, but at any rate you can give the House of Israel a good name.

Perhaps a sign like they used to hang out at the Barn Stormers' performance of Macbeth in the Western States would be appropriate for me to put up:

"Don't shoot! He's doing the best he can!"

CHAPTER X

1. An incurable optimist at the front.
2. I knew we were to be punished by the stripes of men.
3. "But we have forgotten God! We are too proud to pray to the God who made us."
4. Isaiah's message to the Brith Colony of Hebrews in the British Isles.
5. Gentlemen of the cloth cannot sidestep or duck this question.
6. Westminster coronation stone was Israel's throne and house of God.
7. A new world brewing; the new era.
8. Where unionism falls down.
9. Why the Turk is Edom of the Bible.
10. General Allenby's campaign was foretold three thousand years ago.
11. He lead God's battle axe in Palestine.
12. Will university professors be selected as fishers of men.
13. Higher critics fail to get "my goat."
14. What the old lion and the young lions did in Palestine in answer to prayer.
15. Armageddon is coming soon.
16. The world has to reap what the world sows.
17. What H. G. Wells does not know about our Bible.
18. Business men with their good horse sense will see God's plan.

CHAPTER X.

Do you wonder that during the late war—when almost everyone at times lost heart and felt that we were nearly at the end of our tether—I never for one moment felt that we would not win! I was the incurable optimist!

At the Front a half-brick diet was my more or less constant companion, mostly deserved for breaking rules and the King's regulations while endeavouring to push on with roads. One compliment paid me I remember. After the Armistice, when every officer's record, ability, capacity, and usefulness had to be placed on paper and sent to the War Office, my record was sent to a certain major-general, and he endorsed on it:

> "A splendid organizer of Labor,
> A Fine Roadbuilder
> Constant in Adversity
> And wise in counsel."

That was going pretty strong for a regular soldier not given to sprinkling sugar on your army rations. But the main thing was "Constant in Adversity," and I could be constant in adversity, because I believed the God-inspired words spoken

THE DESTINY OF AMERICA

by the prophets, and I believed God meant just what they said He did. Goodness knows, there was room for a few optimists in the fall of 1917 at Paschendale and in the spring of '18 in front of Amiens!

I knew Israel was to be punished in measure by the stripes of men, and we certainly got an overflowing dose, but no more than we deserved, and no more than was necessary to bring all the nations of Israel to their knees in prayer and humiliation, asking for the help of the Almighty God. From that time on we went forward until we won.

However, we still worship idols and golden calves, idols of wealth and idols of fashion and popularity; idols of ease and comfort and the movies! We nationally waste much substance in more or less riotous living; we have food almost to burn, while sections of Europe and Asia are dying by the millions, without causing us to turn a hair; yet they are our brothers.

Abraham Lincoln in a proclamation to the American nation, in 1863, after describing the benefits bestowed upon his nation, said:

"But we have forgotten God! We are too proud to pray to the God who made us."

I wonder what Lincoln would say to-day, could he see the nation he was chief executive of fifty-eight years ago. If it was true then that you had forgotten God, then how much more true it is to-day, with the mad hustle and bustle of life in your big cities, and the Lord's Day given over largely to golf, motoring, and pleasure, while the churches with their few hundreds languish.

Well, gentlemen, don't forget that you will have to pay the bill and will continue to do so, if you do not mend your ways, as you did in the sixties; and the judgment for you and your sons and daughters is as surely being ground out by the mills of God as it was sixty years ago before your Civil War, when Lincoln saw it and made no bones of plainly telling you about it in his proclamations to your nation. As Boss Tweed once remarked, when caught with the goods, what are you going to do about it?

For these and other national sins and shortcomings and because of our failure to deal justly, to love mercy, and to walk humbly with God, as your martyred President, Abraham Lincoln, did during his years of service to America, and as George Washington did before him, we will require another term of many years of war to purify our nation and yours, and we will surely get it in Armageddon which still has to be fought; but it will be won as was the late war, with God's help, by His battle axe and weapons of war, with which He promises to smash nations and kingdoms, i.e., by Israel, His chosen servant, "in whom and by whom he will yet be glorified."

1. Listen, O isles [British], unto me; and hearken, ye people, from far [U.S.A.]

3. Thou art my servant, O Israel, in whom I will be glorified.

6. And he said, It is a light thing that thou [O isles and people from far] shouldest be my servant [what for?] to raise up the tribes of Jacob [why the isles if the Ten Tribes were not in them?], and to restore the preserved of Israel: I will also give thee [isles, or Israel] for a light to the Gentiles, that thou mayest be my salvation unto the end of the earth. (Isa. 49:1, 3, 6.)

Now, to every preacher I submit that as the end of the earth is not yet with us, somewhere is God's chosen people Israel who are the light-bearers to the Gentiles. Gentlemen, where are they? Are they in Russia, Norway, Sweden, Denmark, Germany, France, Spain, Italy, Greece, Africa, or Iceland, or where?

This same people must possess all the other marks of Israel, among which are the following:

They must keep the Sabbath.
They must be invincible in war.
They must possess the gate of their enemies,—the sea.
They must be not the least, but the chiefest of nations.
They must possess Joseph's blessings, now in the hands of Britain, U.S.A., and the other Anglo-Saxon nations.
They must have ruling over the nation or company of nations, a King, of the Royal seed of David.

Who are the light-bearers to-day to the Gentile heathen nations? Surely it is none other than the Anglo-Saxons; who, therefore, must be God's servant, Israel.

Now, Gentlemen of the Cloth,—University professors not barred,—it is no use sidestepping this question. Either these statements are true or they are false. If they are true, God's Kingdom is right here on earth with a visible enduring dynasty ruling over it just as foretold to David King of Israel (Psalm 89), and it will continue till Christ comes to rule His kingdom. Moreover, you don't have to die to be of it nationally; every believer in Christ, as St. Paul says, is of Israel. Mr. W. Pascoe Goard in the national message of the Bible writes:

> The Bible knows a threefold presentation of the kingdom of God.
> 1. The universal kingdom of God "The Lord hath set His throne in the heavens and His kingdom ruleth over all." Manifestly this is not the throne upon which David reigned.
> 2. The national kingdom of God on Mount Zion, of which we shall have more to say. This was David's kingdom.
> 3. The ecclesiastical, or spiritual kingdom, of which, for instance, the Lord spoke to Nicodemus. "Except a man be born again he cannot see the kingdom of God." This constitutes the apostolic message of the Church, and with that we shall not deal further.
>
> Regarding the national kingdom of God established upon Mount Zion, let us make enquiry. Of that Kingdom certain general things may be said in order to give direction to our thoughts.
>
> It is not an universal kingdom! It is not a kingdom established at its inception, over all men, nor over

THE DESTINY OF AMERICA

all nations! It is not exclusively a spiritual kingdom, but a national and material kingdom, over which has been set a very material throne!

The purpose of this kingdom of Jehovah among the nations seems to resemble the purpose of Jesus Christ among individual men. It is the enlightener, the leader, the librator, and the savior of the nations. It seems indeed to be God's plan to save men, one by one, through the redemption wrought out by Jesus Christ the Saviour, and to save nations by the ministry of the chosen nation.

What excuse will avail for being a blind leader of the blind when God's Word, which we are told to search, is so plainly written that the ordinary man who searches the Scriptures can read and understand?

How much good will it do you, Gentlemen of the Cloth, to plead: "The higher critics misled me!" Were you, gentlemen, bidden to study the higher critics or to "search the Scriptures"? *You were specifically bidden to find the sheep that were lost,* "the flock of my pasture" and this flock according to the Word "are men"; the Lost Ten Tribes of Israel were His "lost sheep," "his flock." What have you or your church done to find them? Mostly nothing. Well its up to you!

Now here is another waymark. When Jacob was on his way from Beersheba to Haran, he stopped at Luz, and that night he had a wonderful vision of a ladder reaching from earth to heaven and angels of God ascending and descending upon it, and the Lord stood above it and told him his seed should be as the dust of the earth and in his seed all the families of the earth should be blessed and He would be with him and keep him. When Jacob awaked out of his sleep he was much awed, and he said, "This is none other but the house of God" and he not only called the name of the place Bethel (meaning house of God) but he anointed the stone whereon he had slept and called that the house of God. (Gen. 28:22.) So Israel used this symbol to remind them of God's presence. In their travels they took this venerated stone representing to their minds God's house. Iron rings were inserted in either end to slip a pole through, for ease in transporting as they moved, and it was placed in a tent when they rested. A recent examination shows the iron rings to be worn to paper thinness and as it has only moved a few hundred miles since it was brought to Ireland by Jeremiah in 576-8 B.C., all this wear must have taken place during its moving from place to place with Israel before it reached Ireland.

Throughout the Old Testament a stone or rock is frequently mentioned, and considering their regard for the stone which Jacob called God's house, it is not difficult to believe that it was this same stone which was referred to in Exodus 17, when Moses smote the "rock," and this may be what the margin refers to as the "throne of the

The British Coronation Chair built around Jacob's stone which the Bible refers to as the Throne of God, (*i.e.* set up by God.)

Lord" in that same chapter. Again, it is not hard to believe that "God's house" may have been "the throne of the Lord" upon which Solomon sat in place of his father.

Three thousand years later, King George the Fifth sat upon the throne of Great Britain and Ireland and what did King George sit upon when he was crowned? Upon that very stone with the old iron rings much worn through the years of travelling; and it has had an honored place in the Coronation Chair for centuries. In fact, every English, Scotch, and Irish King who has reigned over Israel since Jeremiah took it to Ireland has been crowned sitting upon it—with the exception of "Bloody Mary" (who sat in a chair which had been blessed by the Pope of that day).

To-day it is in Westminster Abbey in Britain under a stone arch upon which is engraven "Surely this is the House of God" and looks out on the graves of those illustrious warriors who for centuries have served as God's battle-axe and weapons of war and have given their lives that God's throne and God's kingdom might endure.

Armistice Day, November 11, 1920, witnessed a spectacle the like of which has never before been seen on this round earth, when our King, as Chief Mourner, our Princes, our Prime Ministers, heads of the Army, Navy and Church followed the remains of "The Unknown Warrior" to his last resting-place in Westminster

Abbey—a fit representative of those hundreds of thousands who gave all they had and all they hoped to be and died in defence of God's Kingdom on earth, not for pomp, vain pride or glory, but for service, service to humanity, service to our weaker brethren and nations, service to the whole world.

> "God of our fathers, known of old,
>   Lord of our far-flung battle-line,
> Beneath whose awful hand we hold
>   Dominion over palm and pine—
> Lord God of Hosts, be with us yet,
>   Lest we forget—lest we forget!
>
> The tumult and the shouting dies,
>   The captains and the kings depart,
> Still stands thine ancient sacrifice,
>   An humble and contrite heart.
> Lord God of Hosts be with us yet,
>   Lest we forget, lest we forget!"

* * * *

This last war our politicians said was fought to end war—but how far from it!

There is going to be a new world as a result of this and the next war, and the makings of this new world and the next war are already in the pot stewing. The "Reds" wish to have this stew flavored with lots of *blood,* blood of the capitalists, the intellectuals, anyone who by merit has lifted himself above the common. Poor deluded people, they know not what they do!

Labor wants this stew inside and out strongly flavored with unionism. "Join our union or you can't work; we won't let you!" High wages, higher wages and short, shorter and shortest hours until they won't have to work at all! They want to say who shall work; of course these chaps who went overseas to save the stay-at-homes' hides—they can't let soldiers, who have served the whole world so well, into the Carpenters', Painters' or Plumbers' Union; they might displace in time some of the stay-at-homes, so Lord Haig's pleading for his soldiers availeth naught. Their unions say it wouldn't do! This is the age when *all autocracies* are headed for the scrapheap, and the labor union that thinks to-day it can hold back fair-dealing with real justice to union and non-union labor does not see what is coming and is riding for a fall. *Brith-ans never shall be slaves! to church, state, labor, or to anyone or anything!* Just now it is unionized labor's turn to see it, to the extent of giving a good day's work with snap and vigor for a good day's pay—which they are not doing, but are slacking.

Some capitalists want theirs and a big slice, and don't give a hoot what happens to the chap below the line. Thank goodness! this class is gradually dying out or giving way and will soon be gone; the good time is coming when every man willing to give real honest work or service for real pay will never want, and that time won't be long in coming.

Unionism has largely spoiled men from giving a good day's work for a good day's pay, in Britain especially, and in America and Canada wherever they can enforce arbitrary autocratic power. "Go slow, Bill" is the general attitude. It was so noticeable when I changed from handling Canadians to handling British labor units on roads in France. Labor fails to see that every man that is slacking on his job is putting a tax on everything he makes and, by raising the price, taxing all his fellow laborers. Union labor cannot live to itself alone, though they act as if they thought they could and often act as if they could lift themselves by pulling on their boot straps. Good will and not strife will eventually be the leaven that will leaven the whole lump, from capitalist to labor with the great millions of people who are between these two warring elements.

Drifting seems to be my "long suit" as I seem to have again left the rails.

Perhaps you will wonder why early in 1917 I told my Jew friend, Major Blank, that we would take the Holy Land and hand it over to his hooked-nosed friends for a national home. I was banking on Rev. Wild, Dr. Poole and statements made in the early seventies and eighties by many other authors on this point about the prophecies concerning these latter days. Ezekiel, who prophecied from 628 to 570 B.C., said:

THE DESTINY OF AMERICA

"I will lay my vengeance upon Edom by the hand of my people Israel." (Ezek. 25:14.) Knowing that we Anglo-Saxon Celts were Israel I knew our job was to take Jerusalem and the Holy Land from Turkey and make a place for the Tribe of Judah to gather together representatively. Esau is Edom, Mount Seir, Idumea, a Gentile nation, and Esau is also Turkey, the Ottoman nation who was to be in possession of the holy places when Joseph-Israel won that land back from the Gentiles, as they did in 1917, just in the 1295 solar years or 1335 lunar years (dating from the Hegira A.D. 622) foretold by Daniel.

The prophecies of Leviticus 26 were also fulfilled in the return of the Jews to Palestine after the land had been laid waste for a period of seven times (a time in the Bible being 360 years), because Daniel, with the other princes, was carried to Babylon in B.C. 603 and Jerusalem was delivered in 1917, just 2520 years later to the year.

Esau and Jacob were twin sons born 1836 B.C. of Isaac by Rebekah. See Genesis 25:23:

> "And the Lord said unto her, Two nations are in thy womb, and two manner of people shall be separated from thy bowels; and the one people shall be stronger than the other people; and the elder shall serve the younger."

Esau was a red man and his offspring, the Turks of to-day, have this same characteristic as a nation. To-day the elder, Esau, is serving the younger, Jacob. It was promised of Jacob's sons "In Isaac shall thy seed be called," and they started out calling themselves Isaac-sons. In their travels, as the Hebrew had no vowels, the "I" was dropped, and on old monuments in the Crimea these Israelites wrote it "Saac-sons" or "Saac-suns" and over thirty other ways, each having the same pronounciation. To-day the word pronounced the same is written in English *Saxons*.

30. "And Esau said to Jacob, Feed me, I pray thee, with that same red pottage; for I am faint; therefore was his name called Edom.

33. "And he [Esau] sold his birthright unto Jacob.

37. "And Isaac answered and said unto Esau, Behold, I have made him [Jacob] thy lord, and all his brethren have I given to him for servants; and with corn and wine have I sustained him: and what shall I do now unto thee, my son?

39. "And Isaac his father answered and said unto him [Esau], Behold, thy dwelling shall be the fatness of the earth, and of the dew of heaven from above;

40. "And by thy sword shalt thou live, and shalt serve thy brother [Jacob]; and it shall come to pass when thou shalt have the dominion, that thou shalt break his [Jacob's] yoke from off thy neck." (Gen. 25: 30, 33; 27: 37, 39, 40.)

Esau hated Jacob with a hatred that has lasted down through the ages for Jacob's seed, Isaac-sons, Saac-sons, Caxons.

"By the sword shalt thou live" has been literally true of the Turks or Ottomans who have crowned their Sultans, not with a crown, but with a sword. But the Master said, "All they that take the sword shall perish with the sword"; and this is still coming true. They have had the fatness of the earth for a dwelling place, the choicest land on earth in their possession and they have made it a desolation from one end to the other.

"And thou shalt serve thy brother." That they did under David and Solomon, and for centuries they held the balance of power as the Sick Man of Europe in the middle East, keeping out Russia, and others, thus serving their brother Jacob (Brith-ish) in a way they did not understand until the fullness of the Gentiles came in and General Allenby took over the Holy Land section of Edom or Turkey.

"And it shall come to pass when thou shalt have the dominion ["Break loose"—R.V.] that thou shalt break his yoke from off thy neck." Here are some facts about the descendants of Esau:

1. In Egypt, the Pharoah of the oppression was a son of Esau in the fourth generation—Eliphaz, Amalek, Thurdan, Rameses. He certainly tried to put the yoke on the neck of Jacob's seed when it was off his own.

2. The Amalekites who attacked Israel after their coming out of Egypt were of Esau origin by Amalek, the son of Eliphaz, oldest son of Esau and his concubine, Timna. (Gen. 36:12.)

3. Haman was of an Amalekitish and Esau descent. He tried to destroy all the Jews and Benjamites, for Queen Esther and Mordecai were both of the tribe of Benjamin, but he was hanged on the gallows he had prepared for Mordecai.

4. Herod the Great was an Idumean, and as King of the Jews when the Romans had dominion over Judah sought the young child Jesus to slay him who was the hope and Savior of Israel.

5. In 1916 Edom, the Ottoman nation, had been in possession of the Holy Land for centuries—but where would they have been had their twin brother Jacob not fought for them against Russia in 1854?*

Edom, O'Theman, or Ottoman has had dominion and lost it and now again Jacob's yoke in the shape of a mandate is on those of them who occupy the Holy Land because the time has come when no nation can live by the sword as Turkey has for centuries past in a Christian land.

"Thus dwelt Esau in Mount Seir: Esau is Edom. And these are the generations of Esau the father of the Edomites in Mount Sier." (Gen, 36: 8, 9.)

---

*History fulfilling Prophecy, by Wm. Reeve.

THE DESTINY OF AMERICA

Esau, as we said before, is also Idumea. Idumea is the Greek form of the name Edom or Mount Seir (rugged) whose original inhabitants were probably for two reasons called Horites—because Hori was the grandson of Seir, and because that name Hori was descriptive of their name as troglodites or dwellers in caves.* Just remember these cave-dwelling habits on the cliffs of the Dardanelles when we come to look over Obadiah's prophecies concerning Turkey.

You will note in the second chapter of Deuteronomy that the Almighty commanded Israel not to molest their brethren of Esau and Mount Seir; they were to pay for any food and drink which they required as they passed through the land in those early days of Israel's wanderings.

Teman, you will remember, is an Edomite, being a son of Eliphaz, son of Esau. A writer in the *Covenant People* for July, 1913, says:

"The Edomite family name Teman in Hebrew is *Th'man* and linguistically identical with *Theman, Althman, Othman, Osman,* or *Ottoman. Osman, Ottoman,* or *Othman* is an Edomite family name. The historian Gibbon in his 47th chapter gives the original form of the name of O'thman, the son of Ertogrul as Thaman; now Teman, or more strictly Theman, was a grandson of Esau. (Gen. 36:11.). And another of the same name (36:42) was one of the dukes of Edom and six times over in the Prophets the name is used for a prominent or leading section of the Edomite race.

Young's Analytical Concordance

"In the very place (Obadiah) in which the destruction of the destroyers of Israel's land is detailed, it is written 'Thy mighty men, O Teman shall be dismayed.' Ottoman is, therefore, the Scriptural designation of the House of Edom in its dominance over Palestine and is a striking testimony of the truth of Holy writ."

Having shown that Teman, Ottoman, and Esau are all Edomite or Edom, as is Mount Seir and Idumea, we can now turn to Obadiah and see what that prophet, who died in 586 B.C. foretold and if it has come to pass.

Ferrar Fenton's Translation into modern English is as follows:

"Thus says the Mighty Lord about Edom;—
We have heard a command from the Lord about Edom
And a message is sent to the Nations;—
'Arise! and go up to the war against Her!'

"Look! I will make you be small among Nations!
And you shall be greatly despised!—
Your bold heart deceived you, who dwell on high cliffs,—
Whose home is on high, and Who says to his heart,—
  'Who can drag me to earth?'"

(Obadiah 1:1-3.).

Now just carry your mind back to the early days of the late war. Britain and France were doing their best to keep Turkey away from her natural ally, of the glittering armour, the great sword rattler of Europe, but those minions of the nether regions, Enver Pasha and Talaat

THE DESTINY OF AMERICA 215

Bey (since gone to his reward!), with the help of the Goben and Breslau switched Turkey to Germany.

Little did they think then or now that they were but the tools carrying out the Almighty's plan for taking the Holy Land from the Ottomans. You may remember how, after much indecision or dilatoriness and delay, Britain decided to send dreadnoughts to bombard these Edomites out of their high cliff forts cut in rock along the cliffs of the Dardanelles and so secure the last gate of their enemies, Constantinople, and also how we had to retire beaten in the task. Had Britain's politicians been students of prophecy and aware that Britain was Israel as was that grand old fighting admiral, Sir John Fisher, they would not have insisted on such a scheme, because the better plan of campaign laid down in the Bible was later practically [and probably unknowingly] followed by General Allenby with such good results by land.

Well, was a message sent to the nations to arise and make war against Edom or Turkey, as specified in verse 1? And has Edom or Turkey been made small among nations in comparison with what she was at the height of her dominion? She will be smaller yet!

The Sultan was the big man among Mohammedan heathendom. But he lost Mecca, Jerusalem, Constantinople and other sacred cities and immense territories and to-day he is "small potatoes" and despised among the aforementioned heathen as predicted in verse 2.

How about verse 3?

> "Your bold heart deceived you [Edom], who dwell on high cliffs [along the Dardenelles],—
> Whose home is on high, and Who says to his heart,—
> 'Who can drag me to earth?'"

After the retirement of our largest dreadnought can you not see the Turks puffing up their chests boastfully saying, "We have defeated the largest ships and the biggest guns in the world, who can bring us down?"

Well, the inspired prophet, Obadiah, 2,500 years ago, said what would happen and declared in no uncertain accents in verse 4:

> "'If with Eagles you soar, if you nest among stars,—
> I will drag down from there,' says the Lord."

And down they came and also their fortifications along the Dardanelles and at Gallipoli.

Verse 7, addressed to Edom or Esau, says (Ferrar Fenton's translation):

> "'Those men, your allies, to your borders have driven;
> They deceived you! Your friends [they] have o'erwhelmed!
> Spread a net on your bread that you did not perceive.'"

THE DESTINY OF AMERICA

The Revised Version puts this verse 7 as follows:

> "All the men of thy confederacy have brought thee on thy way, even to the border: the men that were at peace with thee have deceived thee, and prevailed against thee; they that eat thy bread lay a snare [marg., "wound"] under thee: there is none understanding in him."

Looking back on what the German friends of Turkey did to her, could you possibly have a more vivid and true description of how they misled poor deceived Turkey, whose bread they were eating and whom they prevailed against and under whom they laid a serious wound that Turkey could not possibly get away from and which finally caused her downfall. They did bring her even to the border of Europe and over the border of the Promised Land past the Euphrates, and to the border of destruction.

> 8. "Shall I not in that day, saith the Lord, even destroy the wise men out of Edom, and understanding out of the mount [or high places] of Esau."

The wise men in Turkey who did not agree to fight against their old-time friends and blood relations, Jacob (Britain), were removed from Turkey's government, and wisdom and understanding have been destroyed out of the high places of Esau—from among Enver Pasha and his ruling circle, and their German masters. Wisdom gave place to German hatred with its absolute lack of understanding of peoples and nations other than those made in the German mould. Then there follows in Obadiah a recital of what the Ottomans had done to their brother Jacob and the result to them of their actions.

9. "And thy mighty men, O Teman [now Ottoman], shall be dismayed, to the end that every one of the mount of Esau may be cut off by slaughter.

10. "For thy violence against thy brother Jacob, shame shall cover thee, and thou shalt be cut off for ever.

11. "In the day that thou stoodest on the other side, in the day that the strangers carried away captive his [Jacob's] forces, and foreigners entered into his gates, and cast lots upon Jerusalem, even thou [O Teman] wast as one of them.

12. "But thou shouldest not have looked on, the day of thy brother [Jacob] in the day that he became a stranger; neither shouldest thou have rejoiced over the children of Judah in the day of their destruction; neither shouldst thou have spoken proudly in the day of distress.

13. "Thou shouldest not have entered into the gate of my people in the day of their calamity: yea, thou shouldest not have looked on their affliction in the day of their calamity, nor have laid hands on their substance in the day of their calamity;

14. "Neither shouldest thou have stood in the crossway, to cut off those of his that did escape; neither shouldest thou have delivered up those of his that did remain in the day of distress."

THE DESTINY OF AMERICA

All these things the sons of Esau have done unto their twin brother Jacob from the time Nebuchadnezzar destroyed Jerusalem to Herod the Great and down through the ages. At the sacking of Jerusalem by the Romans they took part in the most hideous atrocities against their own flesh and blood, since which time the mills of God have surely been grinding out the Almighty's judgment as foretold in the following verses of Obadiah's single chapter devoted to Turkey's downfall, and confirmed by Isaiah 31 and Jeremiah 49.

If you read of the sacking of Jerusalem, you will have some idea what Jacob's children had to suffer at Esau's hands. The Armenians in our day have met with a similar fate by Talaat Bey, the Armenian murderer who ordered that they be robbed of their substance and be cut off at the crossways and murdered. But the time of judgment has arrived—the judgment which the mills of the Ruler of the Universe has been grinding out for the O'Themans since then.

15. "For the day of the Lord is near upon all the heathen: as thou [O'Teman] hast done, it shall be done unto thee: thy reward shall return upon thine own head."

Ferrar Fenton's translation puts it:

But the day of the Lord will come on every Nation [not Turkey alone];—

And as you have done, He will do to yourselves;—
Your crime will return on your head!

17. "But upon mount Zion [the hill of Jerusalem] shall be deliverance, and there shall be holiness; and the house of Jacob shall possess their possessions."

Now what are the facts that will enable us to judge if these predictions were just so much east wind or if they were based on an understanding of divine law? Has Turkey's crime turned on her own head? Has the day of the Lord, the day of right and justice as opposed to might, come upon nations? Has there been deliverance upon Mount Zion or Jerusalem? Has the House of Jacob possessed their possessions?

To me all these questions are to-day answered in the affirmative and that without any spiritualizing of God's real promises to Israel, right here on earth. This spiritualizing our blind shepherds find so necessary to use to explain Bible prophecies, because, when they get you sky-piloting and have your feet and your reason off the solid ground and they state that this means that, and that means something else "in the spiritual sense" and in the world to come, you cannot usually argue back, because you don't know, neither do they; they are only guessing, and guessing wrong at that and telling you only what they have been taught, like the doctors who used leaches a hundred years ago and bled everyone— they were wrong, but they knew only what they had been taught. I've never yet heard a churchman, high or low, who could explain God's promise to Israel intelligently, save by this sane and logical identity method. They can all see the propehcies about Judah and the Jews coming true to the letter through real people, some fifteen million Jews; but when you ask them, what about the kingdom, Israel, who were ten times as many, where they are, they hum and haw and say, "Israel is God's church!" Has God's church been the Creator's battle-axe and weapons of war with which he was to smash nations? If so, what nations has the church smashed? Does God's church possess the "gate of his enemies?" If so, what gate, what enemy and where? Has God's church become a nation, a great nation, and a company of nations? Not on your life! And the church never will and never can fulfil those grand prophecies foretold of national Israel, in the isles of the sea. <u>The church sees the Cross of Christ but fails to see that He left His Kingdom on earth to His ten servants, the Ten Tribes of Israel, my chosen, My dispersed, My outcasts, My sheep, My witnesses, Mine elect, My nation, My servants and My people Israel who were to *"occupy"* until He comes.</u>

In my humble opinion, the allwise Creator caused the Bible to be written for the common ordinary everyday variety of men and women whom Abraham Lincoln said God must have loved because he made so many of them—just plain folks. We, not particularly the parsons or University professors, are bidden to search the Scriptures and to read God's Word. Surely then, that Word that we are bidden to search is understandable by the ordinary man—we, us and company—else why are we bidden to read it? Abraham Lincoln when he was without education read it by the light of a pine knot and absorbed into his very soul the wisdom contained in its pages.

In one of the messes I was in, in 1917, we were blessed with three Oxford graduates, two of them parsons, one a don; and believe me, the higher critics had nothing that Oxford in their day had not swallowed hook, line and sinker! They were chuck full of it, and yet, they used to lament the condition of the church—as if you could grow oaks from thistle seed! I often wondered how they expected to inspire Tommy with faith in the Bible that they were in doubt about themselves. They lacked what they tried to pass on to the army, faith.

I used to console myself with the fact that when the Master was on earth, there must have been the Oxford professors of that day, though I failed to remember his having picked any of them to carry his Gospel to the people and to be the light that was to lighten the world. Rather he

THE DESTINY OF AMERICA

chose fishermen, and carpenters and tax collectors to be his fishers of men. It is possible, and I think most probable, if my mess mates were fair samples, that when He comes again to His Kingdom right on this earth, this time to rule, and when His feet in that day stand on the Mount of Olives and it cannot be so very many years ere He does this—for He is coming in just the same manner that he went,— it is possible that Oxford and many seats of so-called higher education will have much to answer and some of them will be lucky if they don't get a goat tag tied on them because so many of our students when they go through our Universities have lost their early belief in our Bible being inspired by the Creator and Ruler of His Universe.

I remember once being asked by one of these Oxford chaps if I really believed that Christ was coming back to this earth. I said,

"Well, what does the Bible say? 'Ye men of Galilee, why stand ye gazing up into heaven? this same Jesus, which is taken up from you into heaven shall so come in like manner as ye have seen him go into heaven.' (Acts 1:11.) Sure, He is coming back to this earth and He is coming back this time to rule His Kingdom of Israel and we Anglo-Saxons are Israel," I said.

The glance of surprise mixed with pity that he bestowed on me expressed his feelings fully; a man who thought as I did was too simple for this enlightened age. They (the Oxford bunch) know so much better than that now, that it was not worth while discussing further the matter with a chap like myself. Higher education should enable men to see God's goodness to all those who ask for His guidance and help, but many students going to our seats of higher education lose much of the faith they had, after a few years there.

Well, I'm thankful I never knew enough for the higher critics to get "my goat" and I still retain my absolute belief in the Bible and the more sure word of prophecy contained therein, because anyone can see prophecy becoming history year after year just as foretold.

Well, again I am drifting away from my theme and in danger of getting "het up." Let's go back to Obadiah!

"The house of Jacob shall possess their possessions," The whole of the Promised Land from the Nile to the great river Euphrates, the territory promised to Abraham, has now floating over it the ensign of Jacob, the Union Jack. This land promised to Israel is possessed by Britain. Are we then not Israel? Judah (the Jew) is joined to us under King George V. of Brith-ain (Covenant Land)—and they shall be no more two people.

THE DESTINY OF AMERICA

18. "And the house of Jacob shall be a fire, and the house of Joseph a flame, and the house of Esau for stubble."

Stubble is straw that has had the grain and top cut off. It still stands up, and Ephraim, Joseph, is the flame to consume it as they did after the Turk was chased out of Jerusalem. Ephraim, Britain, was like a flame among the stubble, burning them up all along the line until the Turks quit fighting and got an armistice; but the end of Turkey is not yet. She will be finished with many others at Armageddon.

Did it ever strike you as strange that neither France, Italy, or Belgium sent troops to help in the campaign in the Holy Land? It was left to the British alone, as it was in 1882, when they took the Egypt end of their possessions, to possess their (Jacob's) possessions—though America should have and will yet come in on it as she did in 1882.

The Ephraimites always had trouble with their H's. See Judges 12:5 and 6 where it cost them the lives of forty-two thousand because of this peculiarity. Not being able to pronounce "Shibboleth," they all said Sibboleth and it is a strange thing that down through the ages that characteristic has stuck to the sons of Ephraim. The cockney of London will say "horanges" and

" 'orses" to this day and it was the cockneys of London who took Jerusalem and who held it, and they are Ephraim, the English, who were to be the head of the tribes, this stubborn stiff-necked people with the bull's head emblem under which they marched when Moses brought them out of Egypt, and now known as Brother John of the Isles.

Even the Word of God must be confirmed by two witnesses. Obadiah mentioned that when Esau should have dominion, he would break his brother Jacob's yoke from off his neck and he did. Jeremiah 49:2 predicts: "Then shall Israel be heir unto them that were his heirs, saith the Lord." Read that whole chapter through as it confirms Obadiah, they being contemporaries. Well, Israel to-day is heir to what the Ottomans had in the Holy Land.

Ferrar Fenton translates Jeremiah 49: 19-22 as follows:

"See he was like a lion coming up from the swelling of Jordan to the permanent meadows: 'I will be sly with them,' he said, 'I will assail from behind them, —what hero can defend them? for who is equal to me, and who expects me? and what shepherd can stand before me?'

"Therefore hear the intent of the Ever-living, which He intends against Edom, and the plans He has planned against the people of Theman, if they do not withdraw the young of the flock; if they do not put them in the Fold.

THE DESTINY OF AMERICA

"The earth shall shake at the sound of her fall;— the voice of his shriek to the Sea of Weeds!

"Look! He comes like an eagle, and flies! and spreads his wings over Bozrah,—and the heart of the heroes of Edom in that day will be like the heart of a woman in terror!"

Well, Jeremiah wrote that description of how Israel was to take this land before 597 B.C., and strange as it may seem, the troops of the old British lion were sly in exactly the manner predicted. They broke through and assailed the Turks from behind and took the heart out of the sons of Esau. In Jeremiah's day there were no aeroplanes, yet with the vision of the prophet and seer, he looks forward 2,500 years and says: "He shall come up and fly as the eagle, and spread his wings over Bozrah"; and our fighting units with their flying squadron attachments did just that and uncovered the hidden places of Esau.

And yet unwise people pooh-pooh Bible prophecy!

You will remember that Turkey at Germany's staff suggestion, started a campaign for the taking of Egypt and of the Suez Canal from Britain. Look up Isaiah 31 for a description of that campaign.

1. "Woe to them that go down to Egypt for help; and stay on horses, and trust in chariots, because they are many; and in horsemen, because they are very strong; but they look not unto the Holy One of Israel, neither seek the Lord!

2. "Yet He also is wise, and will bring evil, and will not call back His words: but will arise against the house of the evildoers, and against the help of them that work iniquity."

Well, the workers of iniquity and their helpers who banked on their numbers and strength, were the recipients of woe ere they got back from that good sized expedition.

3. "Now the Egyptians are men, and not God; and their horses flesh, and not spirit. When the Lord shall stretch out His hand, both he that helpeth shall fall, and he that is helpen shall fall down, and they all shall fall together.

The Egyptians who were stirred up into revolting and the Germans and Ottomans who went down to help them all fell together in that particular "show."

4. "For thus hath the Lord spoken unto me, Like as the lion [the old British Lion] and the young lion, [Australia, New Zealand, etc.] roaring on his prey, when a multitude of shepherds [leaders or generals] is called forth against him, he [the lion] will not be afraid of their voice, nor abase himself for the noise of them: <u>so shall the Lord of hosts come down to fight for mount Zion and for the hill thereof.</u>

5. "As birds flying, so will the Lord of hosts defend Jerusalem; defending also he will deliver it; and passing over he will preserve it."

Well, reader, what is the answer to verse four?

THE DESTINY OF AMERICA

Like as a lion, the old British Lion and the young lions which came from Australia, New Zealand, etc., to help the old lion redeem Jerusalem, were not afraid of the multitude of shepherds or generals opposed to them; but like lions all, they went for the Turks and their Hun masters, and they certainly put the fear of God into their hearts after their first encounters. *How Jersalem Was Won,* written by W. T. Massey, who was with Allenby's army, gives a splendid account of it. So did the Lord of Hosts "come down to fight for Mount Zion and for the hill thereof."

I cannot do better than quote from the *Covenant People,* November, 1920, issue, extracts from a lecture by the Rev. Commander L. G. A. Roberts, R.N.

"The Word of God is true! 1917 is exactly seven times [the times the prophet foretold] from the Babylonian captivity of Judah, and in that year the Holy City was delivered. Obadiah gives you exactly the strategical method in which their deliverance took place. Isaiah 31:5 tells you exactly how God delivered it 'As birds flying, so will the Lord of Hosts defend Jerusalem; defending also he will deliver it; and passing over he will preserve it.

"When General Allenby came over the Mount Gerizim—the Mount of Blessing—the Turks were fleeing over Mount Ebal—the Mount of Cursing.

"When Allenby came to Jerusalem the Turks were convinced that the Holy City never could be taken because it had been predicted that, unless the waters

of the Nile flowed into Palestine, the Turks would
hold Jerusalem. What occurred? When crossing the
desert our gallant engineers laid a water-line—a pipe-
line from the Nile—right across the desert, and near
Jerusalem, they connected it through into the Holy
City. When the Turks saw the fulfilment of their own
prophecy—the waters of the Nile mingling with the
waters around them—they knew all was lost.

"The Arabs had also a prophecy. They said that
Jerusalem would one day be delivered by the hand of
a Prophet of God. General Allenby's name, in Arabic,
is "Allah-Nebi,' which means a 'Prophet of God.' These
two things coinciding the Turks were quite nonplussed.

"Remember how Jerusalem was taken. General
Allenby did not want to fire a shot at the sacred city.
He telegraphed home to the Premier to know what he
should do. Bombard Jerusalem or not? The Premier's
reply was that he must be left to do as he thought
right. That did not satisfy Allenby. He telegraphed
home to the King and the King told him to make it a
matter of prayer. Well, they had a service; the
whole of the officers went to prayer. As they were
rising from their knees a herald from Jerusalem arrived with a flag of truce, and the Governor of
Jerusalem surrendered to the British forces.

"'Before they call I will answer, and while they
are yet speaking I will hear.' 'Call upon me in the day
of trouble and I will deliver thee and thou shalt
glorify me.' What was the result? Instead of going
into Jerusalem like that proud Kaiser, General Allenby went in as if he understood it was a Holy Mission,
on his feet in humble submission.

"It was not he or the British army, but the act
of God; and Allenby went in, not for the conquest of
Jerusalem, but for its deliverance.

THE DESTINY OF AMERICA

"Now the Turks were very sorry they had left and thought they would come back. They placed their guns and prepared to bombard. Suddenly the areoplanes appeared, and then the Turks finally retreated. Not a shell was fired against the sacred city.

"That date [1917] is stated in the Pyramid."

We have God's two witnesses, the Bible and the Pyramid and both were correct. We have also God's two national witnesses who bear the Union Jack, the older glory, and the other "Old Glory," the Stars and Stripes; and the nations they represent will continue to be used for God's glory throughout the world.

W. T. Massey writes:

"The troops of the Turks and Germans who were entrenched on the hills beyond Jerusalem, when preparing to attack it were told that when Jerusalem was recaptured they were all going to have a free day to do as they liked in the City and so we saved Jerusalem from being pillaged."

On December 27th the Turks delivered thirteen attacks towards the city for the purpose of capturing it; but the British gained seven miles in these attacks, and the end of the day found Jerusalem defended by four strong lines so they made true the words of the "Unseen Strategist of the Universe"—"Defending also he will deliver it; and passing over he will preserve it."

In the face of this absolute fulfilling of prophecy how do men doubt the reality of God's promises to His servant, Israel, who was to win the Holy Land and who did win it in the year and in the manner predicted in those prophetic words describing how the Lord would defend and deliver Jerusalem, the city of which it is written in 2 Kings 21:4: "In Jerusalem will I put my name." These words were uttered over 2,520 years ago and in 1917 they came true, seven "times" from the destruction of Jerusalem and the taking of Judah captive.

What does this mean to you? Since these material, earthly, and national promises dated for 1917 and all previous dates have been fulfilled, what about those for 1921, 1922, and 1923, and so on to 1936 when Armageddon is to be finished? You can depend upon it that every divinely inspired prophecy from 1917 to 1936 will come true and at the allotted time. "The arm of the Creator is not shortened." "Behold, he that keepeth Israel [and we are Israel] shall neither slumber nor sleep."

George Washington, Abraham Lincoln, and others of your wisest leaders have told you in their national proclamations what God has done for America, and you let it slide like water off a duck's back. How much are you doing towards

THE DESTINY OF AMERICA

carrying on your share of the Creator's work? You have a large share to carry on, for you are a large part of His executive nation and company of nations and there are punishments which you or your children will receive just as surely as the sun rises if your share of the job is not performed.

Good thoughts that are not transferred into good actions are not worth two hoots in the hot place. If the foregoing statements are facts, then you personally have a job, a divine job, that you cannot pass over to your parson's shoulders. He is already overstocked with troubles and doubts of his own just now, since the German higher critics are in the discard.

Armageddon will be upon us about eleven years from the time we took Jerusalem. We will need in that day a United Empire and a United States free from hyphenates, though there are world-wide forces to-day at work internally and externally trying to disrupt both these mighty nations who are destined to carry "good will" to the whole world. They were both given the divine commission to "push the people together to the ends of the earth" and they have been carrying it out and will continue to do so, imperfectly of course, but still heading in the right direction.

The late Colonel Theodore Roosevelt, that outstanding American and apostle of good will, whose autographed photograph I am proud to look at hanging on my wall, believed that the man who was opposed to cultivating the warmest friendship between the Anglo-Saxon nations was no friend of the world.

Let us carry on the divine command with truth, justice and good will to all men, pushing peoples together, first among the English-speaking peoples and continuing until the whole world is one in aim.

There are papers and institutions in all countries devoted to stirring up trouble and strife between us. Knowing that their aim is to breed "contention," let us not reply in kind, and when you see quoted in a paper a strife-breeding paragraph against your nation, just remember the class of people who are interested in propagating that strife and smile and remember that One greater than all has His hand on the helm, even if you and I do not and cannot understand the why and the wherefore of all "the mystery of God."

How many men do you suppose there are in the steel business who understand what is going on in the mind of that master of steel, Charles M. Schwab—even men helping him to run his big plants? Then what about His workmen, how can they understand the Master Mind? Should we, then, be surprised that so few know and understand the Creator's plan? They ask why He permits wars, famine, pestilence, and social disturbances, forgetting that the prophets saw and foretold that just these things must come to pass as the result of the nations not carrying out His laws which have never been abrogated, as were the ecclesiastical laws, but which were confirmed by Christ when he was on earth and they have been waiting ever since for our Israel nations to accept.

The world has got to reap what the world sows; they can no more duck it than they can stop the sun from shining. The hatred of Prussian Germany against God's chosen people, Israel (The Anglo-Saxon-Celts) dates from the time they took Hebrew Israel captive 720 years before Christ, so 'tis fairly well ingrained. Russia has been taught for years by those apostles of light and Soviet learning—Lenine and Trotsky (organized in New York and sent through Germany)—to hate the Covenant men, the Brith-ish (and Americans are as much Brith-ish as are Canadians), with a hatred that will not die, but will continue until they are almost wiped out at Armageddon; but there will be enough left to take the news back to their people, that God not only rules in heaven, but also on earth as in heaven and that the Christ has come again to rule.

Germany was pretty busy through all the underground and above ground channels before 1914, stirring up strife between us all and preparing for *"der Tag."* Prussia, Russia and other unseen forces to-day are busier than ever before along the same lines in India, China, Persia, Turkestan, Egypt and all the uneducated heathen nations. Prussia is prohibited from doing anything by the sea because of the navies of Britain, United States and Japan, and so that genial advocate of "good will on earth" (?) Von Tirpitz by name, advises the U.S.A. to build a big fleet of dreadnoughts, hoping that some day the Huns may be able to stir up strife between America and Britain and have them destroy each other—when Germany would step into "her place in the sun" that we hear so little about these days. Before your big and growing navy is complete you will be again harboring the German type of embassy with Von Bernsdorf and Von Papen attachments for blowing up your munition plants and stirring up Mexico and Japan to attack you.

The papers last week reported a certain Hugo Stinnes as buying up manufacturing plants in Russia. Prussia will eventually reorganize Russia. France will see that they do not manufacture armaments in Germany, but she cannot prevent her from doing so in Russia and all the Armageddon war material required will be made in Russia.

The Bible says the Army of the Chief Prince of Rosh are all to be mounted on horses, and it is interesting to note that in 1901 Russia had thirty million horses, America about eight million and the rest of the world about eight million, so the "Chief Prince of Rosh" and his millions will not have to hoof it as we did in Belgium along the pavé.

I think the "day of the Lord" is come upon all nations and the almost unexpected wiping the slate clean of licenses for men to sell firewater and the prohibiting of its being openly drunk in the United States and Canada is a definite mile-post showing how near is the approach of that "great day," because ere that day many things that offend have to be put into the discard.

Still again I've drifted from my text. The prophet Isaiah said:

> 8. "Then shall the Assyrian [Prussian] fall with the sword, not of a mighty man; and the sword, not of a mean man, shall devour him: but he shall flee from the sword, and his young men shall be discomfited.
>
> 9. "And he [the Assyrian] shall pass over to his strong hold for fear, and his princes shall be afraid of the ensign, saith the Lord [what ensign?], whose fire is in Zion, and his furnace in Jerusalem." (Isa. 31:8, 9.)

Did these things come true? Did the sword of General Allenby (unknown as a "mighty man," and not a "mean man") devour the Hun and Turkish troops? and did the Huns pack up and beat it back to Germany, their stronghold for fear, leaving poor Turkey to fight it out alone, which they proceeded to do? The history of this campaign shows these verses have come true to the letter.

"And his princes [German or Prussian] shall be afraid of the ensign [that grand old covenant banner which was to be set up, the Union Jack], saith the Lord, whose fire is in Zion." "And the house of Jacob," said Obadiah, "shall be a fire"—to burn up Edom, or Turkey, (for he says the house of Esau shall be for stubble) so that they could "possess their possessions in Zion," and, according to Isaiah, the Lord said this ensign whose fire is in Zion (our Union Jack which Jacob sets up), will make the Assyrian or Prussian princes afraid. Certainly it did put the fear of God in their hearts when they saw it floating over Jerusalem. See Isa. 11:12:

> "And he shall set up an ensign for the nations, and shall assemble the outcasts of Israel, and gather together the dispersed of Judah [the Jews] from the four corners of the earth."

It is also predicted in this chapter that the envy of Ephraim (the English) should depart, which will be a fine thing for Britain, when Judah will no longer vex Ephraim, because the "international Jew" has given Brith-ain (Covenant land) many a sore touch and has vexed Hebrew Ephraim (Britain) more ways than you have fingers and toes. When all of Hebrew Judah works together with Hebrew Ephraim instead of partly with the Prussian Assyrian, their ancient enemy, for whom the "international Jew" worked during the war, a change will come over Jewry the world over.

I have been interested reading Mr. H. G. Wells' articles, entitled *The Salvaging of Civilization,* in the *Saturday Evening Post.* He like many authors, Sir Philip Gibbs included, cannot see daylight out of the present troubled world conditions and suggests, as a partial improvement, rewriting the Bible, because he thinks its not up to date. Its too redundant, too much information about minor Kings of Israel and Judea, too much Obed begat Jehu, etc., etc., and it doesn't say anything about modern history! Too bad, isn't it, and nothing about elections!

Well, when Mr. H. G. Wells can write a condensed history of the world covering over 4,000 years and can foretell accurately what will happen to nations and people from 2,000 to 3,000 years before it does happen; when he can accurately foretell the work the American and British sections of Israel will do several thousand years ahead of the time they are to do it, then, and not till then, should he have the temerity to rewrite the Bible.

Because Mr. Wells does not know or understand why the redundancy in Leviticus, why the information about minor Kings of Israel and because his pulse stirs feebly over the date that Nathan begat Zabad, etc., is not a good or a logical reason for cutting them out, but is rather a reason why Mr. Wells should study why they were put in.

One might as well argue that because junior students do not understand the books of Euclid when they read them over, therefore, they ought to be scrapped!

There are probably a whole lot of things Mr. H. G. Wells does not understand about other things as well as the Bible, but to my unsophisticated mind that does not appear a good reason why they should be scrapped but rather why we should study them and become more proficient in knowledge about them.

I may be wrong, but it seems to me that before any man, even with the abundant knowledge Mr. Wells may possess, decides that he or a committee should meet and trim down our Bible, which has been handed down through the ages, they should first read the last chapter of Revelation and the warning contained in it as translated by Ferrar Fenton which is as follows:

The Last Solemn Warning.

"I certify to every one listening to the statements of the prophecy of this book—If any one shall make an addition to it, God shall lay upon him the plagues which are recorded in this book; and if any one shall take away from the statements of the book of this prophecy, God will take away his portion from the tree of life, and from the city of holiness described in this book."

Men who place themselves on a par with the divinely inspired prophets of old who wrote our Bible, which has proven so true down through the ages, and who think it can readily be improved by their scissors, paste pot, and pen have an opinion of their qualifications that, to say the least, would not be condemned for modesty.

Mr. H. G. Wells agrees that the Bible has held together the fabric of western civilization which could not have come into existence and could not have been sustained without it; but he says it no longer grips the community, so he'd scrap parts of it and chuck in some up-to-date "stuph" compiled by modest prophets like himself!

Is it the fault of the community that the Bible no longer grips it? or is it the fault of the Bible? This same Bible gripped Oliver Cromwell and the men of all ages when the Anglo-Saxons everywhere were at their best. It gripped George Washington, it gripped Abraham Lincoln, and it has gripped every great leader the English-speaking world has ever had—this same old-fashioned Bible. The wisest men down through the ages have absorbed wisdom from its pages, and to-day it will grip men who study it with a stronger grip than it has ever had before, because to-day they can see how its prophecies have been fulfilled in the British Empire and the United States of America; and they can see many things that our forefathers took by faith that have now been made facts of present day history in national Israel—facts which can be seen plainly, though most people condemn them before they have given ten minutes to study it.

The power that is to rule the world—which Mr. Wells discusses at length—was settled and ordained thousands of years ago and given by the Creator through the mouths of His Hebrew prophets to Israel. Mr. Wells writes about the foundations of a world state, and discusses pro and con whether it should have a president or a king. If he knew his Bible better he would know that these questions were decided and settled thousands of years ago. There will be a world state. Its foundations were laid thousands of years ago in Jerusalem. "In Jerusalem will I put my name." (2 Kings 21:4.) A king will rule this world state and Christ will be that king and Britain and America will be large factors in that world state.

Mr. Wells refers to "that strange book, the Revelation of St. John the Divine, it comes to an end, it leaves off in the middle of the Roman Imperial and social conflicts," etc. Now the facts are that it does nothing of the sort. The Book of Revelation is exactly what it professes to be. It reveals or is a Revelation in synopsis form and in Hebrew symbolical langauge of the world history from the time of Christ's appearance on

THE DESTINY OF AMERICA

earth, when he was crucified, until he shall come again to His Kingdom on this earth.

Further, when Mr. Wells understands his Bible better, he will find that there is not a question before any nation or nations to-day, neither of elections, independence, self determination nor anything else that is not amply provided for in our present Bible without its being added to or scissored away. Bibles are so cheap—yet so little read in the so-called Christan nations of to-day that they fail to grip; but that is the fault of the people who do not study them. They contain all the wisdom of the ages, and there is no single question that I know of on the political horizon to-day that cannot be solved, properly and permanently solved, by applying the laws laid down in its pages.

President Harding understood this when he was sworn in with his finger on the passage:

> "What doth the Lord require of thee, but to do justly, and to love mercy, and to walk humbly with thy God?"

If people would only get it into their heads that the large world problems are being worked out by Israel according to God's plan and that the Creator has His hand on the helm! The Brith-ish commonwealth, because it is not an Empire, and her offspring would have been on the scrap heap ages ago but for the guiding hand of Providence time after time; and this same unseen hand will continue to protect His chosen people, the Anglo-Saxon-Celts, in the future, provided they continue to seek the help of the Almighty God from whom George Washnigton and Abraham Lincoln sought daily help and received it in full measure.

When we had our back to the wall in front of Amiens, and every Anglo-Saxon nation the world round sought God's help, we received it in full measure and our arms prospered and we won through.

Would to-day that we had a Moses in Israel, who would speak unto the people "that they go forward," as when the Red Sea was in front of them and Pharaoh behind, they went forward dry shod. Moses adhered to the plans laid down by God. Would that our leaders and your leaders could see God's national plan, adhere to it, and go forward! Then would God prosper your undertakings, as your Great Seal proclaims to the world.

Gentlemen of the short-haired variety, its up to you for decision! If you will apply the horse sense and reasoning business ability you use daily, to this subject, you can absolutely wipe out sickness, disease and poverty in Anglo-Saxon countries by working to the Creator's plan and you can permanently solve every question now troubling your nation and the whole world. Isn't that a desirable basis for even the highest grade captains of production to aim for?

IN CONCLUSION

As one looks over the field of foreign affairs in so many nations and sees the vain strivings, leading in many cases to headlong national destruction, one wishes at times there was a power that would take some of our Secretaries of State for Foreign Affairs by the hand and instill some of this wisdom and light contained in our Bible into their perhaps not unwilling ears.

How many Secretaries of State in the world are there, do you suppose, who realize that God the maker and ruler of this Universe laid down his plan in His Book for them to follow? How many men in the Cabinets of the world know there is a plan laid down for them to hew to? Don't all answer at once! Yet . . .

When the Most High divided unto the Nations their inheritance, when He separated the sons of Adam, He set the bounds of the people according to the numbers of the children of Israel. For the Lord's portion is His People; Jacob is the lot (Cord.-margin) of his Inheritance. Deut. 32: 8-9.

* * * *

And he hath made of one blood all nations of men for to dwell on all the face of the earth, and hath determined the times before appointed, and the bounds of their habitation. Acts 17:26.

Well it seems to me, that as the Creator has taken the trouble to state that *He set the bounds of the nations and hath determined the times before appointed,* that the wise thing for our Statesmen and Rulers, our League of Nations, etc., to do is to try and learn what that plan is: unless like Lenine and Trotsky with their New York Jewish backers who think they are wiser than Jehovah and will make a plan of their own that will assuredly come to naught carrying with it all the workers of iniquity.

Yet that is unwittingly what we have for ages been trying to do and what a hideous, ghastly failure man-made laws and plans have made of this glorious old world of ours.

Do you realize Mister Business Man that the God of Heaven laid down national laws. Statutes and sample judgments for use on this earth for all the Anglo-Saxon-Celtic nations and they were given by his servant Moses to Israel and that they were given to be used for a thousand generations [which time has not yet elapsed] and that they have never been abrogated except when reviewed by Christ who abrogated one statute, strengthened six and then adopted the whole of the law thus making the commandments, statutes

THE DESTINY OF AMERICA

and judgments an integral part of His New Testament gospel and of His new covenant.

I noticed in an American newspaper some months ago that there were 79,422 new laws passed in America in 1920. I wrote to your Congressional Library to see if they could give me the numbers of laws, statutes and man-made judgments that have been ground out since 1776 and which were still in operation in U.S.A., but he could not say, neither can any one—but—there must millions of them and no one knows or understands them, yet we wonder that people to-day have little or no respect for law.

How could it be otherwise? How can we have respect for what neither you, we nor anyone else can know is the law?

When the United States of America and the other Saxon nations see that they are Israel and adopt Israel's National Constitution, laws and statutes, and follow the sample judgments, all three of which are contained in about 50 pages of the Bible, there will never be any question about the Judges giving right decisions, because anyone can study those pages as well as the Judges, and then you will appoint Judges for and only because of their character and ability to give justice and equity their proper place in the U.S.A.

Speaking to an old friend connected with the law department of one of our governments some time ago, I asked how many laws we were operating under now, how many statutes and how many judge-made decisions that had the force of law did we have?

He could not say (but admitted that law in Canada was in an absolute condition of chaos), neither can anyone else say but there are thousands upon thousands of volumes on hand to dig into and try and find some Judge who has ruled on a point that will help your client. How can we have respect for such man-made law and for the men who to-day are working to make black appear white and who to-morrow are working to make it appear green and the next day to make it appear yellow or whatever particular color that day's client pays them for trying to make it?

Respect? respect for that type of law is dead, dead as a door nail, never to return in this world, but the new Era, thank God, now on the way, will bring back to National Israel its God-given constitution, the honoring of which is again and again insisted upon in our Bible, (the last chapter and last verses in it specifically tell you not to forget the law of Moses) and upon the honoring of that Constitution and the keeping of its statutes, commandments and judgments, hangs the cure for every trouble that to-day afflicts mankind in the United States of America.

That sounds a bit unreal, a bit overdrawn, doesn't it? And yet it is true, Rev. Wm. Pascoe Goard of Vancouver, author of "New Light on

Old Paths," has printed a pamphlet "The National Message of the Bible" that is absolutely astounding and illuminating in what it points out with reference to this matter.

After careful perusal of his basis of argument and the basic facts contained therein, taken solely from the Bible, I have no hesitation in declaring that within 16 years the United States of America as well as Canada, Australia and the Mother Country, will each have repealed all their man-made laws and will nationally have adopted the digest of Constitutional law given to Moses by Jehovah, as laid down in Deuteronomy, in which you will notice there are *no ordnances,* they being ecclesiastical and pertaining to the Altar and the ecclesiastical duties of the Priesthood.

How did this Divine Constitution get mislaid after it was given to Israel? Well, Jeroboam, whom you will remember as the first king of the ten tribes of Israel, abrogated the ecclesiastical law, and Omri, one of his successors, tiring of Jehovah's digest of laws and statutes put them aside, so causing Israel to sin, and then legislated to suit his own ideas (Micah 6:16), since which time the laws and statutes of Omri and his successors have ruled the world and a pretty mess they have made of it.

My friend, Henry Ford, would try to correct U.S.A. judgments by paying Judges from $25,000 to $75,000 per annum for passing out judgment, and so make them independent of the big interests, but it won't do Henry. You've got to go back to the basic trouble which is not salary. If your engine is missing: fix your engine, don't waste time playing with the horn (or mouthpiece), it won't get the flivver running. No Judge, I care not how able he is, can assure anyone *Justice* under the present system or lack of system of man-made law, "so scrap the lot," its the only remedy that will bring results, and *take on those unchangeable eternal laws laid down for us, applicable both on earth and in Heaven, which can no more be changed than can the immutable laws of nature laid down by the same author.*

What has it cost America for not taking on and obeying these immutable laws? Well I am certain that it is many billions of dollars each and every year that you are giving the go-by.

The principles of right action, as Mr. Goard points out are few: "They are all included in the Constitution, they cannot be changed, added to, or repealed: they are each one illustratively applied in the Constitution; therefore, the Constitution is perfect in our age and is capable of full application under our complex life."

* * * *

Constitutional legislation belongs to God only and whenever a man or nation claims the right to make laws, whether autocratic or demo-

THE DESTINY OF AMERICA

cratic, he or it is trespassing upon the divine prerogative, for *God has not trusted men or nations to make laws for the government of their fellows.*"*

Now you wise men of all our governments who are turning out the everlasting grist of Omri-made laws by the seventy-nine thousand per annum in one nation, which no one knows about, which not one in a hundred thousand would understand if they knew of them, and which no one obeys. Suppose you take a day off and study those simple laws laid down in the 50 pages of our Bible for we-us-and-company the Anglo-Saxon-Celtic nations and all others who will take them on.

If my friend Samuel Gompers and the American Federation of Labor, which he has guided so ably these many years, would put a little time in on this subject they would get the sure remedy for all poverty, for all sickness, for all disease, that now bears so hard on millions of the working people in America: because most of us work on this continent.

How many hundreds of millions of dollars do you spend in county, state and federal hospitals for the sick, for the blind, for the insane, etc., every year in the century? And how many billion of dollars have been permanently invested in the

---

*The National Message of the Bible.—*Wm. Pascoe Goard, Vancouver, B.C.*

buildings for these necessary [at present] public institutions?

What does it cost America, in hundreds of millions per annum for cattle diseases, for hog fever, for tubercular cattle, for ticks, for the boll weevil, for wheat rust, for the corn borer and the hundreds of other blights and things that afflict this present generation?

What is Afflicting America?

Listen you cool-headed business man and you more hot-headed leaders of labor and you chaps now being ground between the upper millstone of Capitalism and the lower millstone of Autocratic Unionized Labor.

The cure for all your ills has been awaiting your acceptance three thousand years—but ye would not. Look up Deut. 7: "Thou [Israel] shall therefore keep the commandments, and the statutes, and the judgments which I command you this day to do them." Verse 15: "And the Lord will take from thee all sickness .... and will put none of the evil diseases of Egypt upon thee."

Then see, in chapter 28, the benefits that would accrue if we kept these laws and statutes and the troubles that would afflict us if we did not keep them. Verse 1: "And it shall come to pass if thou shall harken diligently unto the voice of the Lord thy God to observe and to do all his commandments which I command thee this day that the Lord thy God will see thee on high above all the nations of the earth."

Then are shewn all the blessings due law-keeping Israel.

Well! We have not kept them but have been running along since Omri's time under man-made laws of several million sorts. No one knows how many! and one is entitled to ask if we have received the punishments promised and due us for our neglect along this line.

In verses 16-22 some of the curses or disabilities under which we shall labor are specified and it is due us to look into them and see if we are afflicted by them in America and Anglo-Saxondom, at this time; because, if we are, the remedy is so simple that the nation, were it so minded, could correct all sickness, all disease, both of man and beast; all influenza, all consumption and all poverty through-out the land in very short order.

In verse 22: "The Lord shall smite thee with a consumption, and with a fever, and with an inflamation, and with an extreme burning, and with the sword, and with blasting, and with a mildew; and they (or these) shall pursue thee until thou perish."

Well gentlemen there they are! Consumption at the head of the list, the white man's plague. Have we got it? and got it bad? "With a fever." Hay fever claims its victims by the million and our cities and farms are afflicted with scarlet, typhoid and other fevers like smallpox, diphtheria, etc. Over 50 per cent. of our population is afflicted with catarrah of various kinds, and so on down the line.

These and other diseases are pursuing us until we perish by the hundreds of thousands. Take the "Flue" alone, it killed more people than the Great War. As foretold, we have acquired all the penalties mentioned by Moses fourteen hundred and fifty years before Christ.

"It is well to note that these physical troubles are not associated with the system of worship but with the system of government, and also that the punishments are physical and not spiritual," and it would seem possible for the nation to accept the divine challenge and obtain freedom from all its physical ills.

To-day the whole world is upset by reason of the war debts and the dislocation of trade, and the consequences—exchange troubles. Well, Mr. Business Man, that was provided for in our statute on credits in Deut., chapter 51.

"At the end of every seventh year thou shalt make a release and this is the manner of the release: Every creditor that lendeth *ought* to his neighbour shall release it; he shall not exact it of his neighbour or of his brother *because it is called the Lord's Release.*"

This would seem a pretty fair authority to quote (providing we really believe our Bibles are the word of God) for the settlement of war debts due by France and other nations all over the world, which everyone knows can never be paid. We seem to have adopted it as far as ordinary debts are concerned, which are outlawed after seven years in Anglo-Saxondom.

The highest authority in Heaven and on earth laid down this law for us and for our guidance. I wonder if we will accept it and obtain the blessings pertaining thereto?

The reason why you are to do this releasing of debts is also specified in verse 4, marginal reading: "To the end that there shall be no poor among you," and also in verse 6: "For the Lord thy God blesseth thee, as he promised thee, and thou shall lend unto many nations, but thou shall not borrow, and thou shall reign over many nations, but they shall not reign over thee."

God gave America the natural wealth that Chas. M. Schwab says put her as the foremost commercial nation of the world and God also commanded her to release her debtors every seventh year.

Is America going to obtain her God-given wealth and then duck the obligations laid down for her guidance in our credit statues? Not on your life. Not when she knows it! America responds quicker when her statesmen point the way than any nation on earth. It's up to you statesmen!

Well, gentlemen, that's my story.

Thus endeth the first epistle of the Roadbuilder to his friends in the United States of America, to his friends in France, Britain and the Dominion of Israel beyond the seas, whom he met in those years of service at the Front.

Just note, that the two Frenchmen most responsible for winning the war, Clemenceau and Foch, whose autographed photographs look down at me as I write, both seem to be of Covenant stock from Brittany, where the early Britons settled and where the Normans (Benjamin tribe) invaded, A.D. 1000, and nearly all the French Navy are Britons. I wonder how many more? Israel was to be among all nations and, after Armageddon, was to be drawn from the North, South, East and West to Jerusalem. I think all nations who have the Lion of Judah on their national coat of arms are portions of Israel,

If there are things herein that hurt, kindly bear in mind that they were written with the best intentions and with good will to stir people, parsons and professors to action and not to give pain. If some of these words seem to bite and sting, kindly look them over and see if it is not the facts that hurt, facts that are, but should not be, that give pain.

My most candid critic, my "better half," says I am too hard on the English and Scotch. Well, my mother came from Suffolk, England, of Norman or Benjamin (the light bearing) stock—hence, perhaps, why I'm impelled to send this, my candle of light, and in a small way try to help light the high road for wandering feet. My father came from Glasgow; so, I have no natural prejudice against my own forebears from the Isles. Being an optimist and Scotch, I have hopes that I've not wasted my time and my winter holidays as well, for I have spent my spare hours and days for the past year writing, rewriting and rearranging this material by hand. If you haven't grasped and absorbed the fact that national Israel's history is foretold down through the ages in our Bible and that the Anglo-Saxon-Celts fill every particular prophecy, and that we are the Israel of the Bible, I sure have misspent my time.

I feel, however, like the optimist who fell off the fifty-fifth story of the Woolworth building in New York, as he was falling through the air he shot past a friend who was standing at his open office window on the eleventh story and was heard to say, "Well, I'm alright so far!"

I would like to put this book into print used by the blind, and present every soldier of the late war who lost his sight fighting for God, for freedom, and for his country, with a copy of it, so that each blind soldier in America may know and understand the part he took with Israel as God's battle axe and as His weapons of war, to bring peace to this trouble-stricken world.

May I sign myself

THE ROADBUILDER,

October, 1921.   Toronto, Can.

All books referred to herein can be purchased:

In Great Britain: The Covenant People, 14 Fetter Lane, London E. C.-4.

In America: A. A. Beauchamp, Copley Square, Boston, Mass.

In Canada: Albert Britnell, 815 Yonge St., Toronto, and British Israel Society, Vancouver, B.C.

APPENDIX

WHAT OF JAPAN?

If Americans knew their future as laid down in the Bible they would fear Japan as little as they now do Canada, Australia, or New Zealand, because the Samurai and up, or the white Japanese, are apparently our own people of Joseph's seed who dwelt in Samaria, hence their name, Samurai.

These Samurai, like the New England stock in America, have always ruled and are as thrifty, high spirited and liberty-loving as are the Americans or the English. They possess all those sturdy characteristics that your Forefathers of Brith-ish stock possessed and I do not wonder that their blood boils when for years they have been referred to as a "yellow" race, by Pro-Germans and your trouble breeding yellow sheets, as well as this year by some people and newspapers who should know better. The Samurai are no more "yellow" than are the citizens of your Southern States, black, though the labor in the South is done by the colored sons of America, so also in Japan the labor is performed by the Malay peoples or Yellow Japanese, but that does not make the white folks of the Southern States black any more than it makes the white peoples of Japan yellow. If the Americans in the Southern States were referred to and talked about as black men by Europeans, they would then understand how these Japanese (who can trace their descent farther back than can one in a thousand of American or English-speaking peoples) feel when they are spoken of and about as an inferior and "yellow" race and as a "yellow peril."

The Samurai records show they came from Eastern Asia over 2,600 years ago, about the time the Ephraim Tribe dwelt in the City of Samaria, which was the capital of the Ten Tribes, hence the prophets often refer to the Ten Tribes as Samaria. The City was 42 miles north of Jerusalem, built 925 B.C. by Omri, and the inhabitants were carried away captive to Media by Shalmaneser B.C. 720. Rev. W. H. Poole, on Page 453,* gives details of a tombstone found in the Crimea—"To one of the faithful in Israel, Abraham-ben-mar-Sinchah of Kertsch, in the year of an exile 1682, when the envoys of the prince of Rosh Mescheck came from Kiow to our Master, Chazar Prince David, Halah and Habor and Gozen, to which place Tiglath-Pileser had exiled the sons of Reuben and Gad and half the tribe of Manasseh, and from which they have been scattered throughout *the entire East even as far as China."* This date the 1682nd year of their captivity equals A.D. 961 and shews that portions of Israel were known to be scattered as far as China.

Another tombstone inscription of nearly 1,000 years earlier states, "This is the grave of Buki, the son of Isaac, the priest, may his rest be in Eden at the time of the deliverance of Israel. He died 702 of our Captivity." This would be about 19 B.C. Hundreds of these tombstones have been found in the Crimea on a high and dry ridge lying east of Sebastopol, on the road from Balaclava to Batshiserai, where there is an Israelitish cemetery in close proximity to a fortification called "Israel's fortress" and the entrance to this spot still bears the name the Valley of Jehoshaphat.

Professor E. Odlum, M.A., F.R.C. Inst., etc., who for many years lectured in Tokio University, has given thirty years' study to this question and is enroute to Japan to make further studies along these lines, is certain that these ruling families and their offspring of the

---

*Anglo-Israel, W. H. Poole. Albert Britnell: Toronto.

WHAT OF JAPAN?

white Japanese, the Samurai, are from the same stock as we Anglo-Saxon-Celts.

In support of this the Professor points out that they trace their descent from the same mother that we do, The Princess of On, whom Joseph married in Egypt. They have among their oldest heraldry the Lion and the Unicorn of the Ephraim Tribe (English) the tribe from which they sprang. They have Moses' fiery serpent of the desert among their ancient relics. In one of their ancient temples they have an exact replica of The Ark of the Tabernacle and once a year with much ceremony the Priests of the Temple carry this ark on poles shoulder high, down to the water, stretch their feet over the water and as it does not divide, they return the ark to its resting place in the inner court of the Temple until the next year. They have forgotten now why they do this, and have done it year after year, down through the centuries, the reason thereof having been lost to the present day priests.

Their Shinto religion he finds after much study to be practically the Hebrew religion of the Desert where Moses lead the children of Israel for 40 years.

In parts of Japan, far removed from routes of tourist travel, once a year the people are commanded by the priest to stay in doors on a certain night because the evil spirits are abroad and as a protection against same, the aforementioned priest sprinkles the door posts and lintels with a red vegetable stain so that the evil spirits will "pass over." I wonder where their forefathers first practised this rite?

If interested readers would look up in the Encyclopedia Britannica, 11th Edition, from page 206 on they would find therein that the Japanese have every outstanding characteristic possessed by Anglo-Saxons and which to-day you claim as typical of America.

May I enumerate a few of them?

Page 208. "Frugality, fealty and filial piety— these may be called the fundamental virtues of the Samurai."

"Essentially a stoic, he made self-control the ideal of his existence, just as do our unexpressive, unadvertising, Englishmen and also New England Americans.

Page 209. "The Samurai entertained a high respect for the obligations of truth. "A bushi has no second word was one of his favorite mottoes," just as was and is the Quakers aye and nay in America.

Page 222. The Shinto religion signifies *The Divine Way.*

"Shinto may be said to be entwined about the roots of Japan's national existence. Its Scriptures, as the Kojiki must be considered—resembles the Bible in that both begin with the cosmogony."

Page 252. "Japanese annals represent the first inhabitant of Earth as a direct descendant of the Gods."

Page 220. "While adopting from Confucianism the doctrine of filial piety the Japanese grafted on it a spirit of unswerving loyalty and patriotism and believed that in the life beyond the grave the duty of guarding his country would devolve on every man." . . . the universally underlying principle was "serve the country and be diligent in your respective avocations!"

Page 222. "Purity and simplicity being essential characteristics of the cult, its shrines are built of white wood absolutely without decorative features of any kind. . . . . "there are no graven images."

This is striking evidence that in the land from which they originally came images must have been forbidden. To whom but our own people have graven images always been forbidden the same now as they were 2,600 years ago in Samaria. If they were pagan peoples graven images would be their long suit.

The tenets of the Shinto creed divided itself into two doctrines that seem fairly close to our own.

Page 209. Says the tenets of the Shinto creed divided themselves, broadly speaking, into two doctrines, "Salvation by Faith and Salvation by Works." What pagan land did they get this from? What heathen people ever had those beliefs as their national religion?

WHAT OF JAPAN?

Page 206. As in Israel and in America so in Japan, every stalwart man had to bear arms at least as early as the 8th Century. The early English were the greatest long bowmen of Europe: Saxon bowmen won our wars and it was the same in Japan. "The bow was always the chief weapon of the fighting men in Japan. War and bows and arrows were synonymous terms" . . . . "Next in importanec to the bow came the sword, which is often spoken of as the Samurai's chief weapon, though there can be no doubt that during long ages it ranked after the bow" as it also did among the Anglo-Saxons."

Page 207. "The Japanese never at any time of their history used poisoned arrows: they despised them as depraved and inhuman weapons", wherein they differ from a more modern nation of alleged highest Kultur who poisoned men by the thousand, yet we and you accepted Prussia on the basis of what our universities claimed for her and her damnable higher criticism, and where did our Professors of Science and Religion land us with their blind acceptance of those "Made in Germany" doctrines.

Page 207. "Although ambuscades and surprises played a part in all strategy, pitch battles were the general rule and it was essential that *notice of an intention to attack should be given* by discharging a singing arrow. Thereafter, the assaulting army, taking the word from its Commander, raised a shout of Ei! Ei! to which the other side replied, and the formalities having been thus satisfied, the fight commenced. "Generosity to a defeated foe was one of the tenets of the Samurai ethics"; where outside of their Anglo-Saxon brethren will you find generosity to a defeated foe practiced, even in these days?

Page 212. It is interesting to note from the Encyclopedia that Queen Victoria in 1858 presented Japan with one quarter of the nucleus of their first War fleet. . . . . I wonder why? Can it be that blood is thicker than water and that as John Bull was in Manilla Bay to help just when wanted, so our Queen helped Japan to her feet when she was in swaddling clothes, so to speak, and we have stood by her ever since as Japan has stood by us, because the word of Japan's statesmen is the equal of our own.

Page 273. "The intense pride of the Japanese in their nationality, their patriotism and loyalty, arise from their history, for what other nation can point to an Imperial family of one unbroken lineage reigning over the land for twenty-five centuries. Is it not a glorious tradition for a nation that its emperor should be descended directly from that grandson of "The great heaven illuminating goddess" to whom she said, "This Japan is the region over which my descendants shall be the Lords. Do thou my august child, proceed thither and govern it." *Go! The prosperity of thy dynasty shall be coeval with Heaven and Earth."*

That almost sounds like the promises made to David that his seed shall endure as the sun and the moon before him.

Well reader, here are all these facts that seem to favor Professor Odlum's belief that Japan was, and therefore still is, a portion of Israel who took council among themselves when they were captives of the Assyrians saying, "let us go into a far country where never yet men dwelt that they might there keep the commandments that they had not kept in their own land." I have wondered if Isaiah, Chapter 41, which was directed to the Brith Colony of the Isles or Britain, might in verse 25 refer to Japan, also of the Isles, located in the north and towards the sun-rising, and they have on their banners the rising sun for a totem or waymark? The verse reads:

"I have raised up one from the North, and he shall come: from the rising of the sun shall he call upon my name; and he shall come upon princes as upon mortar and as the potter treadeth clay."

WHAT OF JAPAN?

If the Samurai of Japan are of Israel from Samaria, then they are of Joseph's seed to whom was given the material blessings and material wealth and the commission to settle the waste places of the earth and to whom also were given the heathen for an inheritance, then I submit is Japan entitled to take on her share of settling these waste places of the earth adjoining her bailliwick, provided she carries out the God-given instructions of governing with truth and justice that Israel was commissioned to carry to the ends of the earth.

By their fruits ye shall know them! Suppose we examine Japan from this angle. This is still the Divine method for judging men, churches and nations. Let us forget the German-made propaganda made against Japan since the day she defeated Russia at Port Arthur, from which day Germany saw a possible rival in the East and commenced to holler "Yellow Peril" and her minions have been at it ever since, and to-day thousands of our best citizens, as well as yours, believe all the true and all the false things said about Japan by those paid employees of the Von Papen brand of Germans. Where was Japan in the late War? How long did she take to get into the game? These were the fruits she brought forth then and I believe she will do likewise in Armageddon our next, greatest, and last war.

What if Japan is a part of Israel? then who are we to deny her that share of God's blessings promised to Joseph's seed, because "when God divided unto the nations their inheritance, he did it according to the numbers of the Children of Israel" who were to be scattered among all nations, and if Japan be of Israel stock then room must be found for her or she will find it and take it as God's purpose cannot be defeated; all sections of Israel must have room to bloom and grow properly.

America, Canada and Australia do not desire that Japanese immigrants be allowed to enter their ports (at present), though Israel was instructed by the Creator to keep their national doors open to all. America has been the melting pot for all nations. To-day she allows Jews from all countries under heaven, good, bad and indifferent, to enter her ports and overflow her cities; and she refuses to receive the clean, thrifty, saving, and hard-working Japanese, who largely works on the land, permission to enter. . . . I wonder why?

There must be some unpublished reason why the type of Jews who fill the poorer quarters of your big Eastern Cities are preferred as immigrants to the clean, energetic, long-hour workers on the land where workers are so scarce and where more production is so badly needed to keep the working men fed, and such the Japs have shown themselves to be in California and in British Columbia as the vegetable growers in those sections.

For years I marvelled at the fear expressed by America's papers and politicians at little Japan's designs in the Pacific until I realized 'twas made in Germany to keep Japan from reaping the fruits of her victory over Russia. Germany had intended taking the Philippines after your nation won them from Spain, in the same way she took areas in China after making Japan give them up, and that was why the German fleet steamed into Manilla Bay when Admiral Dewey had taken the Islands. Japan having had this humiliating experience does not propose in future to be in such a feeble condition on the sea that any nation can force her to give up what she is honorably entitled to possess.

Japan would have as much chance in war against the U.S.A. as a Ford flivver would have in a head-on collision with a ten-ton Packard truck; the fliver might dent the radiator in front but that would be the beginning and end of the damage done, while it would be smashed in the head-on impact and run over by the truck and the Japanese are wise enough to see that, and I believe they have no more idea of fighting with U.S.A. than has Canada your northern neighbor.

If Japan is a section of Israel then she as much as we, was promised the heathen for an inheritance and the waste places of the earth, and we should therefore treat her accordingly and judge her by her fruits, and by her past performance of her engagements.

As another way-mark of where Japan is heading I noted in a *Boston Herald,* Sept. 15, 1921, issue, that learning to read English is now one of the requirements in Japanese schools and so it is being taught in all Japanese schools. Only ten per cent. of Japanese are illiterate, a much lower percentage than war tests found in America in 1917. When Japan acquires English how long will it be before she nationally adopts our Bible and becomes our Brother in language and ideals?

The U.S.A. years ago served notice by one Munroe to all European Nations "Hands Off America." Has Japan not quite as much right to-day to say to the world "Hands Off Asia" and if not, why not? America had a Bible authority for her action in that respect. What if Japan has the same authority? Japan does not treat her engagements as scraps of paper. She came to the world's assistance in the world's hour of need. She did everything she was asked to do, did it surprisingly well and was willing to do more, and now we are told America has asked Britain to throw her friend of yesterday overboard after using her and not to renew the treaty she has with her comrade in arms, Japan, and the present mouthpiece of Canada's Government says "Me Too." But John Bull, Australia and New Zealand are in the right this time and will, I think, prevail and a renewed treaty made with, I hope, the U.S.A. included.

During the war, when Canada, Australia, New Zealand and South Africa asserted their right as equal partners in the Brith-ish Commonwealth of nations and were granted the same, the nation to object was their brother, the United States of America, who had had to fight against and not for Great Britain to receive the same rights, all of which were God-given rights laid down thousands of years ago and now being put into practice.

America fears five votes to one when, as a matter of fact, the chances are that the younger nations of the Commonwealth (because it is not an Empire governed from a central point) are much more apt to vote with U.S.A. and against Great Britain, as all these young nations have a freedom of thought and a vision of the mind that is given to but few Englishmen in the tight little Isle, but is characteristic of the broad acres of the U.S.A., Canada, Australia and South Africa.

At any rate they are nations the equal of and as self-governing as is America.

Yet America stood against our signing the Peace Treaty and to-day we are not invited to take part in the November 11th disarmament conference, unless invited by Britain to make up part of their delegation. In other words we can only get in by crawling under the protecting wings of Mother Britain as little chicks do under the mother hen.

How long will it be ere Brother Jonathan realizes that we are full grown nations with a large following of our own and to ask us to crawl under any sheltering wings is belittling to the dignity that we in common with all other Israelitish nations possess as their birthright.

If Japan is of Israel's brotherhood they must be treated as such or we and you will pay the penalty for standing in the way of the Creator's designs.

If your Government and ours were only wise to what was coming during the next 15 years they would bind Japan to them with bands of steel at the coming conference, because they will need Japan as Japan will never need the U. S. A., because if they are not for us they will be against us in Armageddon. I, however, have every confidence in Japan being with us just as they were in the late war.

WHAT OF JAPAN?

Instead of asking Britain to break with her friend who came to the help of the world in the time of the world's greatest need, which is an evidence of who they are, America should join with the Brith-ish Commonwealth of Nations and Japan in a triple open and above board covenant and then all quit building super-dreadnoughts and build ships for carrying aeroplanes instead, and fast up-to-date cruisers, etc., because the time is coming when five men shall chase an hundred, but you must be ready to transport your series of fives in a hurry.

The world witnessed its last big sea war, when the Battle of Jutland was fought in 1917.

THE
British-Israel-World Federation

14 FETTER LANE, LONDON, ENGLAND

Patrons:
H.R.H. Princess Alice, Countess of Athlone.
The Rt. Hon. The Countess-Dowager of Radnor.
His Grace The Duke of Buccleuch, K.T.
The Rt. Hon. The Earl of Dysart.
The Rt. Hon. The Earl of Meath, P.C., K.P.
The Rt. Hon. Lord Gisborough.
The Rt. Hon. Lord St. John of Bletso.
The Rt. Rev. The Bishop of the Falkland Islands.
The Rt. Hon. W. F. Massey, P.C., Prime Minister of New Zealand.

President:
The Rt. Hon. Lord Gisborough.

Secretary-General:
Herbert Garrison, F.R.G.S., F.R.C.I.

Hon. Treasurer:
J. Arthur Jutsum, Esq. (Manager, London Joint City and Midland Bank, Westminster, S.W.)

Among the Vice-Patrons are:
The Marchioness Dowager of Headfort; The Dowager Lady Lurgan; The Lady Wilma Lawson; The Hon. Mrs. Adolphus Graves; Lady Smith Dodsworth; Laura Lady Grant; Lady Pearson; Lady Peirse; Lady Stanley; Rev. J. H. Allen (Bishop W.M. Church, U.S.A.); The Rt. Rev. Bishop Vaughan, D.D.; Admiral Sir Richard H. Peirse. K.C.B., K.B.E., M.V.O.; Lt.-Col. The Hon. Stuart Playdell-Bouverie, D.S.O., R.F.A.; Sir James Outram, Bart., F.R.C.I.; Sir Mark J. MacTaggart Stewart, Bt.; Rev. Samuel Clements, D.D. (U.S.A.); Rev. A. B. Grimaldi, M.A.; Col. Ed. F. Gosset; Col. Frederick Horniblow, C.B.; His Honour Judge Corbet Locke, K.C. (Canada); Col. C. E. R. Mackesy, C.M.G., C.B.E., D.S.O. (New Zealand); Rev. G. H. Lancaster, M.A.; Landseer Mackenzie, Esq.; Rev. W. M. H. Milner, M.A.; Rev. James Mountain, D.D.; Rev. Wm. Patterson, D.D. (Canada); Rev. Mark Guy Pearse; Rev. Arthur Pritchard, M.A.; Rev. L. G. A. Roberts (late R.N.); Rev. R. H. Sawyer (U.S.A.); Rev. J. Anderson Watt, M.A.; Rev. E. J. Wemyss-Whittaker, M.A.; Rev. Dinsdale T. Young; Rev. Philip Young, L.Th.; Professor E. Odlum, M.A., B.Sc.; Col. F. Weldon.

HISTORY FULFILLING PROPHECY
BY WILLIAM REEVE.

The facts of history illuminated by the Bible, the Great Pyramid and the Coronation Stone. The author has some interesting conclusions regarding the measurements indicated in the Great Pyramid.

Price $1.00.

THE KINGDOM OF GOD
BY CHARLES WESLEY EAKELEY

"A gem of a book," says the Roadbuilder.

Price $0.80.

THE LOST TEN TRIBES
BY REV. JOSEPH WILD, D.D.

This work has probably had the largest circulation of any book identifying the English-speaking people with the Lost Ten Tribes of Israel. Many of the prophecies made by Dr. Wild in this book have been fulfilled since its first publication in 1878. The reader will find it most interesting in the light of the events of the past few years.

Price $1.25.

Any of the above books will be sent postpaid upon receipt of order.

A. A. BEAUCHAMP, Publisher
603 BOYLSTON STREET - - BOSTON, MASS.

JUDAH'S SCEPTRE AND JOSEPH'S BIRTHRIGHT—An Analysis of the Prophecies of Scripture Concerning the Royal House of Judah and the Many Nations of Israel, the Lost Ten Tribes.

BY REV. J. H. ALLEN

It is clearly recognized among all thoughtful students of the Scriptures that a profound story is revealed in the history of the Twelve Tribes of Israel, and that this story pervades the Bible from Genesis to Revelation. The author shows by indisputable logic and facts that although the prophecies concerning Judah (the Jews), have been largely fulfilled, those more far-reaching ones pertaining to Israel have not been recognized as applying to any of the nations of the earth to-day.

Price $1.60.

THE NATIONAL REBIRTH OF JUDAH.
BY REV. J. H. ALLEN

In this work the author deals with the prophecies concerning the kingdom of Judah and the restoration of Palestine. He also shows the responsibility of England and the United States in the relationship to Zionism and its ultimate. This timely book is of vital interest, not only to the Jew, but to the Christian as well.

Price $1.00.

THE NATIONAL NUMBER AND HERALDRY OF THE UNITED STATES OF AMERICA.
BY REV. J. H. ALLEN

How many have ever thought of the significance and meaning of the heraldry of the United States as found on its coinage and Great Seal? Yet from the founding of the Republic until these latter days it has been proclaiming its message almost unheard. The day is not far distant when the message in this little book will be taught in every public school.   Price $0.40.

Any of the above books will be sent postpaid upon receipt of order.

A. A. BEAUCHAMP, Publisher
603 BOYLSTON STREET - - BOSTON, MASS.

OUR INVINCIBLE RACE,

or "Israel my Glory"

BY REV. J. H. ALLEN.

This book might be considered a sequel to the author's great work *Judah's Sceptre and Joseph's Birthright* which deals literally with the prophecies of the Old Testament.

A special feature of *Our Invincible Race* is the New Testament evidence that the Anglo-Saxon Race is the Israel of the later prophecies, the race who was to receive the Heaven-sent Word, which it was prophesied the house of Judah (the Jews) were to reject. Upon this house of Israel, because they accepted that divine Word, the Glory of the Lord has risen and has become the promised Light to the Gentiles, to whose brightness the Gentiles have come.

Ready November 15th.   Price $1.75.

Correspondence invited regarding any books upon the question of Anglo-Israel or upon any phases of the subject.

A. A. BEAUCHAMP, Publisher
603 BOYLSTON STREET - BOSTON, MASS.

THE
WATCHMAN OF ISRAEL

A MONTHLY PUBLICATION IN THE
INTERESTS OF ALL ISRAEL.

This magazine is published with the belief that a broad understanding of history and prophecy upon which the identity of Israel is based will revive the spirit and inspiration of Christianity in all denominations.

Thousands of thinking people are to-day awakening to the momentous fact that men and nations are not the creatures of chance and change since there is an unfailing design of God and a divine order governing the destiny of men and nations. The English-speaking peoples of to-day are the lineal descendants of the Lost Ten Tribes of Israel and must fulfill in these latter days the responsibilities decreed for them through the patriarchs and prophets.

Is it not important that our leaders and people acquaint themselves with these responsibilities and with the Bible's message to Israel?

The *Watchman of Israel* is published monthly and contains contributions from the best writers on this subject from all over the world.

Subscription price, $2.00 per Year.
Single copy, 25 cents.

A. A. BEAUCHAMP, Publisher
603 BOYLSTON STREET - BOSTON, MASS.

PRINTED IN CANADA.